When Britain
went to
WAR

When Britain
went to
WAR

By Richard Havers

First published in 2009. A catalogue record for this book is available from the British Library

ISBN: 978-1-844258-42-0

Published by Haynes Publishing, Sparkford, Yeovil, Somerset BA22 7JJ, UK

Tel: 01963 442030 Fax: 01963 440001 Int. tel: +44 1963 442030 Int. fax: +44 1963 440001

E-mail: sales@haynes.co.uk Website: www.haynes.co.uk

Haynes North America Inc., 861 Lawrence Drive, Newbury Park, California 91320, USA

All images © Mirrorpix

Creative Director: Kevin Gardner

Packaged for Haynes by Green Umbrella Publishing

Printed and bound in the UK by J F Print Ltd., Sparkford, Somerset

When Britain
went to
WAR

Contents

"A nation that forgets its pas

There has arguably been more written about the Second World War than any other subject. Tens, probably hundreds, of thousands of books covering every aspect of the conflict from the war in the air to the war beneath the waves; the conflict in the jungles of the Far East, to the North African desert and the battles on the snowy wastes of Russia. Most tell of the incredible heroism of the ordinary fighting man and, in some cases, women. However, there has been far less attention paid to the war on the home front in Britain; a war that involved, in a myriad of ways, every man, woman and child in the country.

The build-up to war was long and when war was declared on 3 September 1939 there was almost a sense of relief. There followed a period of almost no serious action, fewer casualties than predicted, both among the troops and the civilian population. All too soon, in the summer of 1940, the battle arrived in the skies over Britain, followed by a bombing campaign the likes of which the world had not seen before. The heroism of the men and women of London and cities the length and breadth of the country has become the stuff of legend.

The Blitz lasted for so long and people got so used to it that they carried on with a fortitude that is hard for us in our modern, pampered world to imagine. In 21st-century Britain, where every news report is overlaid with adjectives that try to suggest how even some minor transport chaos is catastrophic, we would find it utterly unbearable to live – and let's not forget work – in the conditions that ordinary people faced throughout 1940 and 1941.

as no future." **– Winston Churchill**

At the same time practically every family in Britain had loved ones involved in the fighting. As war spread with the Japanese attack on Pearl Harbor in December 1941 millions of British fighting men were engaged in war across the globe. The worry, the lack of information, the long periods with no word at all made the middle years of the war seem endless.

By 1944 when the tide was clearly turning and D-Day marked a watershed in the fight against Nazi Germany the V-1 rockets began raining down on Britain, killing thousands. Later the V-2 rockets caused further havoc and almost had the British Government planning an evacuation of London.

With the war over there were mass celebrations, but Britain had paid a high price. There was destruction from bombing that would take decades to repair. Over 380,000

military personnel lost their lives in the conflict. A further 67,000 British civilians were killed; nearly as many suffered serious injuries. Naturally these numbers pall somewhat when compared to the German dead and seriously injured; people led by a madman whose power-crazy lust for killing and world domination has never been equalled and hopefully never will.

This book is dedicated to the men and women who fought and died and those who engaged in their own battles without even leaving home – *When Britain Went To War.*

"This country is in the position of a besieged fortress, with every man, woman and child in the front line."

– A judge in 1941 sentencing some food thieves

1938-1939
The build-up to war

In September 1938 Prime Minister Neville Chamberlain flew to Munich to meet German Chancellor Adolf Hitler. It was not the beginning of the long slow march towards conflict, but it did mark a significant shift in attitudes and implied aggression.

"How horrible, fantastic, incredible it is that we should be digging trenches and trying on gas masks here because of a quarrel in a far away country between people of whom we know nothing."

– Neville Chamberlain, September 1938

Neville Chamberlain boarding a British Airways aircraft on 15 September 1938 to fly to Munich to meet German Chancellor, Adolf Hitler to discuss the Czechoslovakian crisis.

Appeasement and Arms

Chamberlain's policy of appeasement towards Hitler's Nazi Germany has been the subject of almost ceaseless historical debate. At the heart of the issue is a feeling that the British Prime Minister viewed much of what happened with detachment, reflecting, perhaps, an attitude emblematic of the age. Alternatively, the cancer that was to be the cause of his death in late 1941 may also have played a part. But Hitler himself had no illusions and is reported to have told those close to him: "If ever that silly old man comes interfering here again with his umbrella, I'll kick him downstairs and jump on his stomach in front of the photographers." The Italian dictator Benito Mussolini shared his fellow tyrant's views; he called Chamberlain "an old man" and "a bourgeois pacifist".

With enemies like that Chamberlain didn't need fellow countrymen, or members of his own party saying, "The Prime Minister has believed in addressing Herr Hitler through the language of sweet reasonableness. I have believed that he was more open to the language of the mailed fist," which is how the First Lord of the Admiralty Duff Cooper vented his anger during his resignation speech on 3 October 1938. This left the field wide open for the arch opponent of appeasement, Winston Spencer Churchill, to

speak out in Parliament on 5 October:

"We have passed an awful milestone in our history, when the whole equilibrium of Europe has been deranged, and that the terrible words have for the time being pronounced against the Western democracies: 'Thou art weighed in the balance and found wanting.' And do not suppose that this is the end. This is only the beginning of the reckoning." **– Winston Churchill, House of Commons, 5 October 1938**

Ten days later Winston Churchill broadcast on American radio: "We must arm. Britain must arm. America must arm, we shall no doubt arm... But arms... are not sufficient by themselves. We must add to them the power of ideas. People say, many people, we ought not to allow ourselves to be drawn into a theoretical antagonism between Nazidom and democracy – but the antagonism is here, now. You see these dictators on their pedestals, surrounded by the bayonets of their soldiers and truncheons of their police. They are afraid of words and thoughts, words spoken abroad, thoughts stirring at home – all the more powerful because they are forbidden... It is the very conflict of spiritual and moral ideas which gives the free countries a great part of their strength..." This was a narrative that Churchill would return to throughout the coming months and a significant step in the "special relationship" between Britain and America.

Prime Minister Neville Chamberlain with
Adolf Hitler.

Neville Chamberlain waves the Munich
peace treaty after returning from Germany
on 30 September 1938

Love and Politics

It was Churchill's powerful notion that focused the minds of many that were involved in pointing the pistol of propaganda at Britain's enemies. Not that everyone who heard the 63-year-old backbencher's forceful rhetoric agreed; at least one newspaper report accused "Mr Churchill, Mr Eden, Mr Duff Cooper, and the opposition leaders of delivering... somewhat truculent and bellicose speeches", while a German newspaper called Churchill "a political tyro".

As 1939 dawned, the newspapers got back to reporting life at home and abroad while of course keeping an eye on the developing crisis. On Monday 2 January the back page headline of the *Daily Mirror* (these were the days before sport was found on the back page of the paper) announced: "Goebbels Disgraced – Losing Jobs". Apparently Dr Joseph Goebbels was beaten up in his Berlin flat for having a fling with a "beautiful married actress". In the previous week the paper had reported that the 41-year-old sported a black eye and bruised face. The woman was Czech actress Lida Baarová, regarded as one of Europe's most beautiful women; the affair had come to Hitler's notice late in 1938. The Führer ordered Goebbels to break off the relationship and remain with his wife and children, of whom Hitler was very fond. Goebbels offered his resignation, which Hitler refused, and then attempted suicide. It seems that this report may have been covering the very end of the affair, just as Baarová was deported to Czechoslovakia.

Goebbels' relationship with Hitler cooled for a while and it has been suggested that the Propaganda Minister's anti-Semitic zeal took even greater focus after this time, leading to the wholesale persecution of German Jews along with those from countries that the Nazis conquered.

With Britain and France on Hitler's list of potential enemies because of their support of Czechoslovakia things remained tense during the early part of 1939. By March, as the weather in the East began to improve, Nazi Germany once again turned its attention to annexing a large part of Czechoslovakia. In the middle of March the prospect of war increased dramatically, and in a speech in Birmingham on March 17 Chamberlain warned the Führer: "I venture to prophesy that in the end Germany will bitterly regret what her Government has done." Germany's actions certainly ratcheted up the feelings of ordinary people in Britain – there were few families who had not lost a loved one just 20 years earlier.

The following day the *Daily Mirror* gave over a full page to Unity Mitford, Lord Redesdale's daughter, who was a friend of Hitler, allowing her to express her views on Germany and the deepening crisis. So that no one was unclear as to its stance, the *Mirror* said: "Would she get the same freedom for unpopular views in Germany? We say NO!"

With statements from Miss Mitford like "As well as being a dreamer Hitler was a realist, and that he only dreamed dreams whose fulfillment he knew to be possible, taking into account his genius for achieving the apparently impossible." She finished her article with the usual rhetoric of the time of those who felt Germany was not bent on war, saying, "I can hardly do better than to end by quoting a passage from the Fuehrer's speech to the Reichstag:

I have stated over and over again that there is no German, and, above all, no National Socialist, who even in his most secret thoughts, has the intention of causing the British Empire any kind of difficulties. From England, too, the voices of men who think reasonably and calmly express a similar attitude with regard to Germany. It would be a blessing for the whole world if mutual confidence and co-operation could be established between the two peoples." **– Adolf Hitler, 20 January 1939**

Four days later the paper was reeling from a deluge of thousands of letters from angry readers, almost all of whom attacked Unity Mitford. Of the many letters that the paper printed this one catches the mood.

BRAVO, Miss Unity! Sure we must work with Hitler. Sure he doesn't want to fight us. I don't want to fight Joe Louis either. Sure we can trust him. A friend of mine had a rattlesnake for a pet. I went to the funeral last week.

Of course he had to protect the Czechs – the Fiji Islanders were working out a plan of aggression against them.

Yes, Fraulein Unity, let's all go to Germany to live. I'll follow you – perhaps.

Roy Galsworthy, Rolle Street, Exmouth.

Unity Mitford (far right).

Home. . .

Undaunted, Hitler wanted Lithuania, Poland, Memel and Danzig to come into the German sphere of influence. Poland refused to subordinate itself to Berlin, and immediately received the support of Britain. At the end of March Chamberlain told Parliament: "In the event of action which threatened Polish independence and which Poland considered it vital to resist, Britain would feel bound at once to lend the Polish Government all support in her power." Over the coming months tension grew, and in May Nazi troops attacked a Polish customs station on the border with East Prussia, adding further to the apprehensions at home.

Meanwhile, Hitler was holding secret talks to secure the agreement of the Soviet Union to partition Eastern Europe on the assumption that Germany would triumph after defeating England, France and anyone else who was foolish enough to stand against the Third Reich. In the public domain of the British media headlines and stories relating to the coming of war increasingly became the norm. Headlines included:

A MASK FOR EVERY BABY

Every child in Britain under the age of two is to have a danger-proof gas helmet, filled with tiny bellows, which the mother can work to supply the child with air during gas attacks.

STATELY HOMES AS CAMPS – ARP PLAN

Country mansions, once the stately homes of England, are to be bought by the Government to serve as centres for Air Raid Precaution (ARP) evacuation camps.

ARP SHELTERS BY HIRE PURCHASE PLAN

SAFETY IN WAR FOR MOTHERS

Expectant mothers who wish to be evacuated from London in an emergency can register themselves at any maternity and child welfare centre.

ALL WORKS MUST HAVE BLACK-OUT PLANS

PETROL RATION IN WAR – PLAN FIXED

It all culminated with the front-page story on Friday 25 August in which the Government passed the Emergency Powers (Defence) Bill, which allowed them to take any action that the crisis demanded.

The Queen at a display of aerial defences including barrage balloons at Hook, near Esher in Surrey, April 1939.

Children from Tyneside being evacuated.

. . . and Away

"Sweeping Increases in Evacuation" ran the headline of 19 May. "SWEEPING increases in war evacuation plans were foreshadowed in the House of Commons last night. Areas containing hundreds of thousands of people may be added to the list of districts to be evacuated. Nine areas formerly scheduled to receive refugees have been taken off the list.

Review of the plans was announced by Mr Walter Elliot, Minister of Health. He said these areas would be taken off the billeting list: – The boroughs of Chesterfield, Dover, Goole, Hedon, Rugby and Scunthorpe. The urban districts of Bolsover, Dronfield, Leyland, and Staveley."

The planning behind the evacuating of children from areas "at risk" was meticulous. On Friday 1 September the first evacuees from London left. The previous day, in a typical piece of Government speak, the BBC warned listeners: "No one should conclude that this

decision means that war is now regarded as inevitable." Schoolteachers, along with MPs, were recalled to their posts, the former to deal with the logistics of a massive evacuation.

Many now think that the evacuation purely involved Londoners, but it also included children, and sometimes their parents, from cities and towns throughout Britain, all of whom headed for the relative safety of the countryside or towns and cities considered less "at risk". Almost 1.5 million left the urban areas in the first three days of September. This number was made up of 834,000

Meanwhile life went on, as this advert from the weekend paper demonstrates.

schoolchildren, and 103,000 teachers, along with over 500,000 mothers and children under school age, plus 13,000 expectant mothers. It was envisaged that the number was going to be closer to 3.5 million.

The people in the country who accommodated the children and the attendant adults were paid by the Government 10s 6d per week (the equivalent of around £73 today, based on average earnings) for taking a child, and 8s 6d for each additional child. This was expected to cover living expenses. If, in addition to a child or children, a mother and an under age child were accommodated, then mothers paid 5s (£35 today) for themselves and 3s for each child, but this excluded the cost of meals. For many the evacuation turned into little more than a few months in the country, with over two-thirds who had left in the September exodus returning to their homes by January 1940. For most it was the lack of a German offensive that took them back home – others were simply homesick. With the beginning of the German bombing raids in 1940 many children, and some of their parents, were once again evacuated.

Children from East Ham being evacuated.

1939
War breaks out

When war finally came there was almost a sense of relief, a release of pressure. Most felt that war was inevitable, so better to get on with it. Initially it seemed as if something really was happening in "some foreign field". The war at home centred around restrictions and shortages and plans and instructions. For many, being told what to do soon wore thin.

"For the sake of history however the facts must be nailed down that the numerous border incidents in Silesia and East Prussia and especially the Polish bombardment of Boynton created a situation which made it incompatible for that serious of military transgressions to go by unpunished. Germany's actions are an act of defence." – German broadcast, 2 September 1939

The Esher ARP in their gas masks.

1939

1 September	Germans cross Polish border
3 September	Britain declares war on Germany
4 September	The RAF attacks German shipping at Wilhelmshaven
5 September	The United States affirms its neutrality
9 September	Advance troops of the British Expeditionary Force (BEF) depart for France where they are deployed along the Belgian border
15 September	German troops surround Warsaw, the Polish capital
17 September	Soviet troops enter Poland
19 September	First British casualty list published
24 September	Food rationing introduced in Germany on small scale
27 September	Warsaw surrenders
	Income tax up to 7s 6d in the £
1 October	British men between 20 and 22 liable for conscription
6 October	Fighting in Poland comes to an end
8 October	RAF shoot down a German flying boat over the North Sea
9 October	Hitler issues orders for the invasion of France and the Low Countries
11 October	BEF on the Continent reaches 158,000 in five weeks
16 October	German bombers attack ships in the Firth of Forth
7 November	The Belgium and Dutch monarchs emphasize their country's neutrality
8 November	A bomb intended to kill Hitler explodes at a meeting in a Munich beer cellar, but the Führer had already left
13 November	German bombers attack Britain for the first time, bombing the Shetland Islands; no serious damage
21 November	Chamberlain imposes an embargo on all German trade, with goods currently in Britain to be confiscated
30 November	Soviet troops invade Finland
7 December	Denmark, Sweden and Norway declare their neutrality
15 December	More British troops arrive in France
18 December	The first Canadian troops arrive in Britain

Lieutenant General Sir John Dill inspecting soldiers digging trenches in France in October 1939 – a scene that looks more like the First World War than the Second.

King-Hall...Page 10

No. 1,277

TWOPENCE

Sunday Pictorial

OUR PREMIER GIVES HITLER LAST CHANCE

"If the German Government should agree to withdraw their forces, then the British Government would be willing to regard the position as being the same as it was before German forces crossed the Polish frontier."

WEAKNESS?

CHAMBERLAIN PROMISES 'NO'

LIGHTNING flashed over a blacked-out London, and thunder rolled ominously as Britain's Cabinet Ministers arrived at No. 10 Downing-st. just before midnight for a suddenly-called Cabinet meeting.

The meeting was the climax of yesterday's mysteries and sensations: above is printed the statement by the Premier and Lord Halifax which bewildered the world.

It followed puzzling last-minute diplomatic moves. The final result —whether it is to be war, and how soon—will be announced by the Premier when the House of Commons reassembles to-day.

Bewilderment started in the House of Commons at noon yesterday. It had been fully expected that Mr. Chamberlain would make a grave statement tantamount to a declaration of war on Germany.

But Mr. Chamberlain was busy talking by telephone with French Ministers.

When at last they heard Mr. Chamberlain speak, Socialists wondered whether Britain was weakening.

Mr. Chamberlain promptly replied, to the relief of the whole House:

" If the House thought for one moment that the statement I have made betrayed the slightest weakening in the attitude either of this Government or the French Government, I SHOULD BE HORRIFIED.

" I share the distrust shown by the House of manoeuvres of this kind.

" I would have been very glad if it had been possible to say to the House now that the French Government and ourselves had agreed to make the shortest possible limit to the time when action should be taken by both of us."

This was a reply to Mr. Arthur Greenwood, who, to the cheers of both sides of the House (and cries of " Speak for England ! ") had said: " This incessant strain must end sooner or later, and the sooner the better."

As M.P.s entered the House newspaper posters announced bombing of women and children in Poland.

At 7.15 Mr. Chamberlain left by car for the House of Commons, and he was followed by Lord Halifax

No reply had yet been received from Germany to our warning on Friday night, said Britain's leaders.

" It is possible that the delay is due to a proposal put forward by the Italian Government that hostilities should cease and that there should be immediately a conference between Great Britain, France, Poland, Germany and Italy."

M.P.'s gasped as Mr. Chamberlain made his statement. In terrible suspense they had waited — lights were dimmed, A.R.P. blinds drawn.

It was expected that the French Cabinet would make its final decision in a few hours,

 So That the People May Know

It Begins. . .

As the sun rose on the morning of Sunday 3 September a fine warm day was in prospect, but, as one writer put it, people in Britain "became tensely calm". The only news to be heard on the BBC was that there was no news; Britain had not received a reply to its ultimatum to Germany. Every one of the Sunday papers had a headline similar in tone to the *Sunday Pictorial*; all had subheadings that included such statements as "Plans For A Long War", and "War Cabinet Ready For Long War; Will Win At All Costs". The BBC newsreaders began to sound as if they were intoning some kind of mantra; people were actually getting restless for something to happen.

At around 8.30am BBC newsreader Alvar Lidell was told to make the short trip from Broadcasting House over to Downing Street where he would be needed to make announcements as the morning's events unfolded. His first job, at 10am, was to tell listeners of what had taken place in Berlin earlier that morning – or, more precisely, what hadn't taken place.

___

"Following the midnight meeting of the Cabinet, the British Ambassador at 9am this morning gave the German Government two further hours in which to decide whether they would, at once, withdraw their troops from Poland. This ultimatum expires at 11am. The Prime Minister will broadcast to the nation at 11.15am."

___

For the next hour or so the BBC played gramophone records, a precursor for what much of the wireless output would be over the coming months. Finally, at 11.15, Neville Chamberlain spoke to the nation.

___

"I am speaking to you from the Cabinet Room at 10, Downing Street. This morning the British Ambassador in Berlin handed the German Government a final note stating that unless we heard from them by 11 o'clock that they were prepared at once to withdraw their troops from Poland a state of war

would exist between us. I have to tell you now that no such undertaking has been received, and that consequently this country is at war with Germany…"

___

He concluded with the words:

___

"Now may God bless you all and may he defend the right. For it is evil things that we shall be fighting against, brute force, bad faith, injustice, oppression and persecution. And against them I am certain that the right will prevail."

___

While no one was surprised by the Prime Minister's announcement, there was now no escaping the fact that the country was at war. How many people read the newspapers that day? Those that did would have found a mixture of the hectoring tones of Government restrictions and instructions along with some mundane and some fascinating stories.

"Black-out or Go to Gaol" read one headline in the *Sunday Pictorial* on Sunday morning. It seemed that many people didn't realize how serious was the need to ensure that no chink of light was to appear through the curtains of homes and offices. In the 20 years since the end of the First World War aerial warfare had become a terrifying prospect. The fighting in Poland had already shown what the German air force was capable of. Even during the First World War over 500 people were killed and almost 1,500 injured in Britain during bombing raids.

New air-raid instructions were issued:

___

"Drivers of horse-drawn vehicles should unharness their horses and if possible lead them to an open space where the horse should be tied to the nearest suitable object. In no case should horses be tied to lampposts or railings. If no open space is available horses should be secured to one of the rear wheels of the vehicle, the halter made fast below the hub of the wheel."

___

Amid all the talk of war there was a report of a "beautiful Mayfair daughter of an English financier"

who was "sacrificing her nationality to wed a German nobleman" and then to live in Germany. Miss Brigid Dunn, daughter of Sir James, was already in Germany where she announced her engagement to Count Peter Wolff-Metternich. According to Mary Dunn, her sister-in-law, the imminent war was the reason for bringing forward their wedding. She added: "The young count is good looking and is a charming person. I don't know much else about him, Brigid has known him for some time."

What happened to Brigid Dunn is unclear, but three years later Sir James and his wife Lady Irene divorced on account of Sir James' adultery with her former secretary.

It's in the Stars

Constance Sharp, the featured astrologer in the *Sunday Pictorial,* had as her entry for Aries (21 March to 20 April), which happened to be Adolf Hitler's sign of the zodiac, the following gem:

"Personal achievement is the keynote of the week! Conscientious work will be recognised and rewarded; your popularity with fellow workers will increase. Good news probably connected with money is also in store. You will feel highly optimistic and very pleased with life, but don't aim too high. Be practical."

Delivering the milk in 1939 in Wooler, Northumberland... not a car in sight, despite the single petrol pump.

Shelter from the Coming Storm

With war declared the press could get down to writing about what was probably going to happen as well as reporting on real events that had already occurred. There were details of the King's message broadcast the previous day along with yet more instructions and orders about what people should and should not do.

"If you have any gold coins you must take them to the bank and sell them to the Treasury. Luxury imports, including motorcars, clothing and perfumery are banned. Residents in Britain must offer foreign securities and bullion, as well as gold coins, to their bankers."

Such announcements marked what would be the start of a long-running theme throughout the war – shortages of goods, and how to find ways to get around the shortages. Not that people could actually do anything to fulfil the order, as Monday 4 September was declared a "limited bank holiday" – which meant simply that the banks were shut.

Meanwhile, the New Zionist Organization called on "Jews of the world to aid Britain, France and Poland in their fight against Hitler". In a prescient call they continued:

"A brutal enemy threatens Poland, heart of the Jewish Diaspora for nearly a thousand years, where over 3 million dwell in loyalty to the Polish land and nation."

When the war was over only around 300,000 of the 3.3 million Polish Jews remained.

There was also a report of the first air-raid alert of the war. At 11.27am on Sunday morning, just as Chamberlain's speech was ending, sirens sounded across London and the south of England in what would have been one of

history's greatest moments of synchronicity – had it really been a German attack. The warning had been triggered by an unidentified aircraft flying at about 5,000 feet over an Observer Corps position at Maidstone in Kent; it was on course for London. Fighters were put on alert, but the aeroplane was soon found to be a French aircraft that hadn't filed a flight plan. "My wife commented favourably upon the German promptitude and precision and we went up onto the top of the house to see what was going on... (there) were already slowly rising 30 or 40 cylindrical balloons. We gave the Government a good mark," wrote Winston Churchill. Some 20 minutes later the all clear sounded, but not before one Londoner is reported to have died of heart failure – the shock of hearing the siren had been too much. Britain had suffered its first casualty of the war. Naturally the rumour mill went into overdrive; some people living in Chelsea told anyone who would listen that the East End had in fact been flattened. Nor was this the last false alarm of the day. The sirens went off again in the evening, and then again at 3am, half an hour earlier in some other parts of the country.

There was no doubting who the enemy was.

Crowds make their way down to an underground shelter as the air-raid siren sounds minutes after war is declared.

A crowd had gathered to hear Prime Minister Neville Chamberlain announce Germany's failure to withdraw from Poland and that Britain had declared war on Germany but they were forced to leave after the first air raid warning of the war.

Life Goes On

Over the coming days the newspapers, along with the BBC seemed to give increasing amounts of space and time to telling people what to do. The Government planned to send a copy of the King's speech to every household, but such was the coverage in the media that in the end this was felt to be both an unnecessary strain on the Post Office and a waste of paper, which was in short supply. Within a matter of a week to 10 days the Ministry of Information published a pamphlet that carried transcripts of all the important speeches by the King, the Prime Minister, and members of the Opposition, as well as a broadcast made to the French by their Prime Minister, Edouard Daladier. Was it information overload?

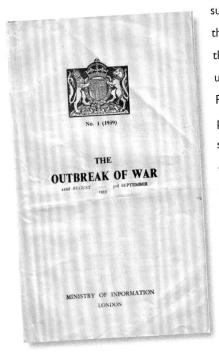

FOOD PRICE CONTROL

IF YOU LOOSE YOUR MASK

But there was also a strong message on what not to do, as the *Daily Mirror* pointed out on 4 September and in similar features over the next few days.

One of the immediate casualties of the declaration of war was the closing of places of entertainment. This led the playwright George Bernard Shaw to write to the newspapers in outraged tones. "May I be allowed to protest vehemently against the order to close all theatres and picture houses during the war? It seems to me a masterstroke of unimaginative stupidity… What agent of Chancellor Hitler is it who suggested that we should all cower in darkness and terror 'for the duration'?" For most of Britain the duration only lasted until the following Saturday when tens of thousands of people "hungry for entertainment cued up outside Britain's cinemas in the 'safe' and 'neutral' areas." The lines were the longest the industry had ever known, but there was a new feature outside the cinemas: large red arrows pointed to the nearest public shelters.

A few days later the film trade were calling for the remaining cinemas be reopened; a strongly worded demand suggested that large numbers of people would be out of work unless this happened. By Friday 15 September every cinema and theatre in Britain was allowed to reopen. The first London theatre to do so was the Golders Green Hippodrome, which actually opened its doors a day before permission was granted.

By Christmas time things were well and truly back to normal, with the pantomime season in full swing. Among those appearing in panto was Pat Kirkwood, "Britain's

WHAT FUEL RATIONS MEAN

BIGGER CROPS PLAN

ALL TO REGISTER – 12 DAYS

Betty Grable" who was starring in *Cinderella* at the Prince's Theatre in Manchester with Duggie Wakefield as Buttons. It was when she made *Band Wagon* with Arthur Askey and Richard Murdoch in 1940 that she earned the Grable tag for her legs. This didn't go down well with the 19-year-old starlet. "It did make me cross. They are simply things to walk around on. I never thought anything more of them than that."

Not so lucky were horse-racing enthusiasts, since the Jockey Club announced that there would be no National Hunt racing fixtures over the coming autumn and winter.

DON'T . . .

THIS is intended for YOU. Read it, remember it, pass it on to your friends. First, and most important of all things is

Don't Listen
to Rumours

You will get all the news that matters—bad or good—in your newspapers. Disbelieve anything else you hear — particularly alarmist news. Next thing to remember is

Don't Broadcast
Information

You may know that there is an anti-aircraft gun cunningly concealed in the field next to your garden. But that's no reason for passing on the information. It may reach someone who should not know it.

Don't Lose
Your Head

IN OTHER WORDS—KEEP SMILING. THERE'S NOTHING TO BE GAINED BY GOING ABOUT WITH THE CORNERS OF YOUR MOUTH TURNED DOWN, AND IT HAS A BAD EFFECT ON PEOPLE WHOSE NERVES ARE NOT SO GOOD AS YOURS.
SO EVEN IF A BOMB FALLS IN YOUR STREET—WHICH IS UNLIKELY—KEEP SMILING.

Don't Listen
to Scaremongers

You will always find scaremongers about. Just treat them as you would a smallpox case—move on quickly. The enemy loves to spread rumours. Part of his campaign was to panic

Britain—and he will still try it, hopeless although it is.

Don't Cause Crowds
to Assemble

THE POLICE HAVE ENOUGH TO DO. IF YOU SEE PEOPLE GATHERING AND THERE IS NO REASON FOR YOU TO JOIN THEM—WALK ON. IN OTHER WORDS—MIND YOUR OWN BUSINESS.
AND ABOVE ALL DON'T FORGET THE OLD ARMY ADAGE.

Be silent, be discreet, enemy ears are listening to you.

NOW GET AHEAD, DO YOUR JOB AND DON'T WORRY.

Food Glorious Food!

The months that followed the outbreak of war have perhaps most famously been called the Phoney War, and, most amusingly, the Bore War. And while it's true that there was not a great deal of actual fighting there was no shortage of things for the media to talk about. Even before the first week of war was over there were rumours that people needed to be registered with retailers to ensure they got food when rationing was in place. The Ministry of Information was quick to jump on the gossip. Mr Morrison, the Minister of Food, announced that rationing would start in about a month and, rather strangely as things turned out, said that, "Rationing does not imply any scarcity of food at all."

It was as early as March 1938 that talk of rationing following the outbreak of war was first mentioned, but the BBC were quick off the mark and their Talks Department were eager to produce programmes about farming and gardening designed to inspire everyone in the art of cultivation. The need to supplement a family's food supply, which would, in reality, be severely diminished by rationing, would be a key feature of war on the Home Front. In the press there were soon stories about food, eating and cultivation that covered an almost endless spectrum of activities.

A week after war was declared the *Daily Mirror* suggested that spades were the fourth line in the defence of Britain.

At first only butter, sugar and bacon were rationed, but by the middle of 1940 meat, eggs, cheese, jam, tea and milk were also rationed. Initially there was some confusion over the availability of supplies. Before Christmas 1939 it was widely reported that bacon was in short supply, while by early February 1940 there was a glut

SPADES—

They're the 4th line of Britain's Defence!

YOUR garden can play a very important part in winning the war.

A plot of ground measuring no more than twenty yards by fifteen can be made to produce at least £10 worth of food a year, enough to keep a family of four provided with vegetables for about six or seven months.

This is how you can help to win the war if you make real use of any soil you have.

You can become the fourth line of Britain's defence.

The more food you can grow, the more ships will be relieved from convoy duty.

Food is just as important as gunpowder; the spade may be as mighty as the sword.

Your First Job

The very first thing to do is digging.

But don't go to extremes and start digging up the lawn and all the flower beds. There is no need for that yet.

What you should do first is to dig, and dig thoroughly, all the vacant spaces you have.

Including any flower beds that are more or less out of sight or have finished flowering.

It's little or no use playing at digging; the job must be properly done if really worth-while vegetables are to be produced. Of the four methods of digging, only two need be described now—single-spit and mock-trenching.

In single-spit digging only the top soil to a depth of about 1ft. is worked.

A trench, 2ft. wide and 1ft. deep, should be opened and the excavated soil carted to the point where the work will finish.

The spade is then thrust vertically into the soil to its full depth 6ins. from the edge of the trench, the soil is lifted and thrown into the far side of the trench, meanwhile being turned over.

It is then broken up with the spade.

The object of the trench—a trench is advisable in all cases—is that it facilitates the burying of manure and annual weeds.

✦   ✦   ✦

In mock-trenching the soil is worked to a depth of 2ft.

A trench is opened in the same way as in single-spit digging.

But the subsoil is forked over to a depth of 1ft., manure being mixed with it if necessary.

The process of digging is identical with single-spit digging, except that when each 2ft. has been worked, the open subsoil is broken up.

Manuring Essential

It's little use spending a lot of time digging if you neglect the vitally important point of manure.

You can't possibly grow good crops without a liberal supply, either natural or artificial.

You will probably find it difficult to get stable manure—this is what is meant by natural—but there are plenty of artificial fertilisers which are equally good.

Among these may be mentioned bone meal, dried blood, meat and fish refuse and hop manure.

Garden rubbish, after it has been allowed to decay, is excellent.

So are dried leaves, and as soon as ever they begin to fall, they should be heaped up in any odd corner of the garden, and it will not be long before they form leaf mould—and everybody knows how valuable that is.

of bacon, so much so that the Government reduced prices by 2*d* per lb (around 10%). Several companies even gave away bacon for nothing to avoid it going to waste.

Also at the beginning of February there was what the papers termed "the Great Meat Muddle". Across Britain butchers were closing their shops because they had no meat to sell. In Sheffield, where "hundreds of homes went without their Sunday joint", butchers decided to close on Monday and Tuesday each week. It was a similar story in Portsmouth, while butchers in Trowbridge and Stratford-on-Avon closed for a day in protest at the poor quality of meat they were expected to sell. This was all part of the complexities of coming to grips with the new circumstances that were proving testing for all concerned. To appease consumers the Ministry of Food announced that they had sourced "cheap and plentiful supplies of dried fruits in the Balkans and Near East".

Page 14 ADVERTISER'S ANNOUNCEMENT THE DAILY MIRROR Thursday, January 4, 1940

MINISTRY OF FOOD

REGISTER NOW FOR MEAT

YOU must register now to enable the Ministry of Food to distribute meat fairly to the shops throughout the country, and to assure YOU of your fair share when rationing begins.

WHAT YOU HAVE TO DO NOW:—

1 Put your name and address on the counterfoil at the bottom of the Meat Page of your Ration Book NOW.

2 Write on the inside front cover of your Ration Book the name and address of your butcher.

3 Take your Ration Book to your butcher and let him write his name and address on the meat counterfoil and cut it out.

4 If you move to another district, take your Ration Book to the Local Food Office in your new district.

5 The numbered coupons *must not* be cut out yet. This will be done by your butcher when you do your shopping after meat rationing begins.

6 If you have registered for meat before Christmas, this registration was unauthorised. You may let it stand, and it will then be effective. Or, if you wish, you may register now with another butcher by recovering the counterfoil from the butcher who holds it and taking it to the butcher you now choose.

YOU ARE FREE TO CHOOSE ANY BUTCHER YOU LIKE

YOU MUST REGISTER NOT LATER THAN MONDAY 8TH JANUARY

AN ANNOUNCEMENT BY THE MINISTRY OF FOOD, GT. WESTMINSTER HOUSE, LONDON, S.W.1

A week later the Ministry announced that more meat was on its way. The argument about supplies weaved around the core decision of who was in charge of processing and distribution. Was it in the hands of people who had dealt with it for years or had it been usurped by the bureaucrats? On a positive note, sugar was not so scarce, though it remained rationed. However, concerning another "staple", it was announced that "the processing of surplus potatoes was going to begin shortly". Fluctuations in the supply of all kinds of food would remain an ongoing narrative throughout the next five years.

During very bad weather at the beginning of February food shortages of another kind made the papers. The chief constable of Lancashire, Captain A E Hordern, rode his horse 10 miles to the village of St Michaels near Preston from Garstang after he received an SOS that read: "St Michaels isolated, No coal, bread or provender." The following day, accompanied by a police inspector, he rode to Calder Valley carrying bread and yeast. With him were three constables, who walked.

Dig for Victory

From very early in the conflict it was recognized that "farming was as important as arming" if Britain was to stand any chance of winning the war. This belief was behind what became one of the most famous slogans to come out of the war – the "Dig for Victory" campaign. As the *Daily Mirror* reported on the evening of 3 October, it all began when Sir Reginald Dorman-Smith, Minister of Agriculture, said on the BBC: "We are launching a nation-wide campaign to obtain recruits to the ranks of the country's food producers. I appeal to you all to dig, cultivate, plant and sow. Let 'Dig for Victory' be the motto of everyone with a garden and every able-bodied man and woman capable of digging an allotment in their spare time."

A week later the paper reported that hundreds of families in Ilford in Essex had put "Dig for Victory" into practice. They were working on wartime allotments recently allocated by the local council. Local school playing fields and areas of some parks were ploughed to make way for the allotments. So it was that Ilford became the "potting shed" of one of the most successful campaigns of the war.

Some people found cause to complain. One letter-writer wrote to the *Mirror* in February 1940: "I'd like to point out that we pay twenty-pole allotment holders rates. I pay 11 shillings and 6 pence a year rent and 2 shillings and 1 penny rates. What about a cheaper allotment campaign before we dig for victory?"

Beg, buy or borrow a spade and Dig for Victory. Not a yard of land must lie idle. To waste land is as bad as wasting food. Dig up your garden. Get an allotment. Grow vegetables that you can store, and keep your family provided for most of the year. Help yourself and help your country.

DIG for victory NOW!

Issued by the
MINISTRY OF AGRICULTURE & FISHERIES, LONDON, S.W.1

DIG FOR VICTORY

Lilliput
THE POCKET MAGAZINE FOR EVERYONE
MAY VOL.6 No.5
7D

It was the perfect way to supplement what would become an increasingly worrisome diet that shortages would impose on Britain. By the spring of 1940 "Digging for Victory" was everywhere; activities were launched right across the country and at local events speakers urged people to give over "a few square yards of garden to the cultivation of potatoes which would produce 45 times as much human food as the same square yards of pasture". This campaign was one of the great triumphs of the war on the Home Front, and by 1943 it was estimated that over a million tons of vegetables were being grown in Britain's gardens and allotments.

Britain Under Attack

On 16 October the war finally arrived in Britain by way of Scotland or, more precisely, Edinburgh, when nine Junkers Ju-88 attacked the Rosyth naval dockyard, on the north shore of the Firth of Forth; it was the first attack on Britain by the Luftwaffe. According to the newspaper reports it was a fairly one-sided affair:

"Between 9a.m. and 1.30p.m., several German aircraft reconnoitered Rosyth. This afternoon, about half-past two, a series of bombing raids began. These were directed at the ships lying in the Forth, and were conducted by about a dozen machines. All the batteries opened fire upon the raiders, and the Royal Air Force fighter squadron ascended to engage them. No serious damage was done to any of His Majesty's ships. One bomb glanced off the cruiser Southampton causing slight damage near her bow, and sank the Admiral's barge and pinnace, which were moored empty alongside. This is the first hit which German aircraft have made during the war upon a British ship. There were three casualties on board the Southampton and seven on board the cruiser Edinburgh from splinters. Another bomb fell near the destroyer Mohawk, which was, returning to harbour from convoy escort. This bomb burst on the water, and its splinters caused 25 casualties. On the other hand, four bombers, at least, out at the 12 or 14 were brought down, three of them by fighters of the R.A.F."

This account does not reflect what actually happened, but as would often be the case during the war, the official and the real versions frequently differed in the detail. At around 2.30pm the German aircraft were sighted, and Spitfires of 603 (City of Edinburgh) Squadron, Auxiliary Air Force, were scrambled from RAF Turnhouse (the

JUNKERS Ju 88A

Wingspan: 59 ft 11 in. Length: 47 ft 1 in. Height: 15 ft 5 in.
Max speed: 286 mph at 16,000 ft.
Armament: Three 7.9 mm machine guns in cockpit and ventral position. Bombload: 3,968 lb.

Daily Mirror

No. 11,139   ONE PENNY
Registered at the G.P.O. as a Newspaper

FIRST BOMBS ON BRITAIN: 4 NAZIS DOWN, CRUISER HIT

Fourteen German bombing planes in a daylight raid on British warships in the Firth of Forth, yesterday dropped the first bombs on Britain since the war began.

The enemy first sent scouting planes over Edinburgh and the Forth, then, in the early afternoon the bombers appeared over the Pentland Hills, dive-bombed the famous Forth Bridge, aimed ten or more bombs on warships anchored off Rosyth, great naval base.

One British warship, the cruiser Southampton, was hit as a glancing bomb struck her bows. Splinters caused 35 casualties among men of the Navy.

Four at least of the German raiders were shot down in flames.

No civilians were killed or injured. No property was damaged. A stray dog was killed by falling shrapnel. In many of the towns round the Forth no air raid warning was given, and for a time officers of the defence forces thought the raiders were British planes.

The Boy Heroes of Britain: A Story to Make You Proud
(See P 11)

35 MEN INJURED IN RAID

OFFICIAL news of the raid, received last night, said:
"Today, October 16, between 9 and 1.30 p.m., several German bombing raids began.

"These were directed at the ships lying in the Forth and were concluded by about a dozen machines.

"The bombers were attacked by our fighters and anti-aircraft guns. At least four enemy aircraft are known to have been shot down, three of them into the sea.

Navy Sink Nazi Warship

A GERMAN warship was sunk in a battle with British ships and planes off the Norwegian coast, according to Schermen who watched the action.

The story is told in the Oslo Tidende at Bergen, Norway. The fishermen returning to the Norwegian mainland from Vaagso Island say that the battle took place Saturday. It lasted for two hours...

Crowds Watch Battle

EDINBURGH men and women watched one of the most thrilling air combats ever seen over Britain.

One Nazi raider, twisting, turning and diving to dodge out of the bursting shells, swooped to within 200ft. of the roofs, then straightened up and vanished behind a hill with the shells still bursting on his tail.

TANKS LOST IN ATTACK

Germans lost more than twenty tanks and suffered losses from 1,000 to 1,500 casualties in yesterday's attack in the Saarbrucken area...

Crashed in Flames

FISHER BOMBERS WERE SHOT DOWN BY R.A.F. PLANES AND CRASHED IN FLAMES AS IT WAS CAUGHT IN THE FIRE OF OUR ANTI-AIRCRAFT GUNS.

"I was sitting at home with my sister when I start, of heavy concentrated anti-aircraft fire..."

Continued on Back Page

were also two people injured on the ground in Edinburgh by falling shell cases.

There is an amusing postscript to the story, which involves a Luftwaffe lieutenant who was taken prisoner after his aircraft was shot down. He was taken to Bletchley Park to be interrogated by British intelligence officers. By

site of modern-day Edinburgh airport) to intercept the raiders. Additionally, Spitfires from 602 (City of Glasgow) Squadron, based at RAF Drem located to the east of Edinburgh, in East Lothian, were on patrol at 20,000 feet.

At around 14.35 hours, the Luftwaffe bombers began their attack and were met with anti-aircraft fire. The Spitfires of 603 Squadron that had taken off from Turnhouse were the first to engage the Junkers and soon shot down one of the bombers. The Spitfires from 602 Squadron were then ordered into the attack and they shot down another. During the action the Royal Navy suffered three officers, 13 ratings killed and a further 44 wounded on board the light cruisers HMS *Southampton* and *Edinburgh*, and the destroyer HMS *Mohawk*. There

all accounts he was the archetypal Nazi, smartly dressed and capable of the full gambit of actions considered de rigueur for German officers. A party of four was assembled for the interrogation, including one of the cryptographers, who were more at home in the halls of academia than questioning a prisoner. The interrogators felt it was vital to adopt an air of superiority and so they sat behind a long table as the prisoner was marched in. He came to a halt, stood to attention and snapped his heels, giving the Nazi salute "Heil Hitler". To which the cryptographer jumped to his feet, saluted and repeated the "Heil Hitler". Realizing his mistake he sat down, or tried to, missed the chair and ended up on the floor. Needless to say the interrogation team learned nothing.

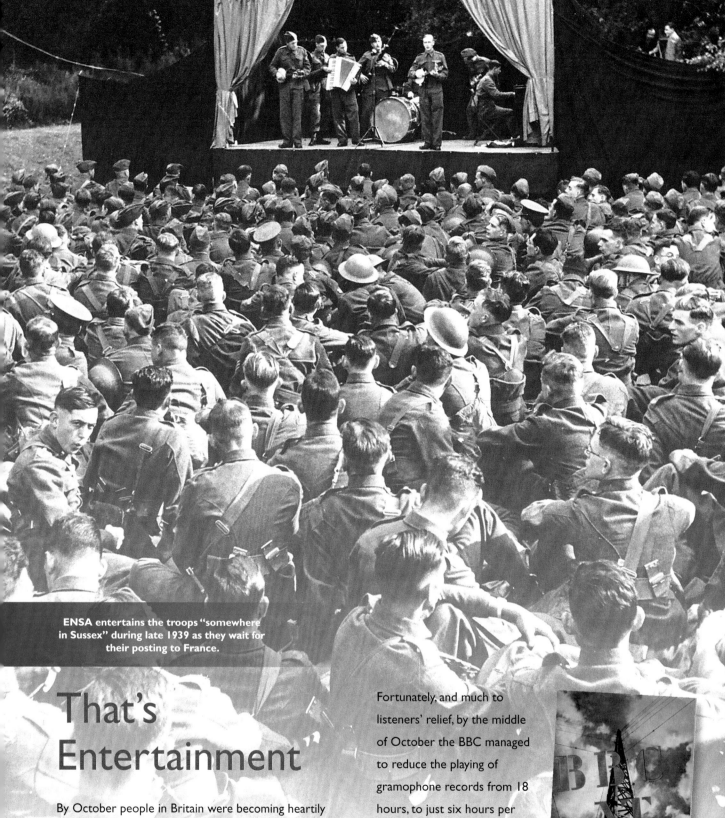

ENSA entertains the troops "somewhere in Sussex" during late 1939 as they wait for their posting to France.

That's Entertainment

By October people in Britain were becoming heartily sick of the BBC's output. News bulletins dominated the airwaves and many of these were accompanied by official instructions as to what people were or were not to do. While these were obviously important, with no real sign of a real war a false sense of security emerged for many.

Fortunately, and much to listeners' relief, by the middle of October the BBC managed to reduce the playing of gramophone records from 18 hours, to just six hours per week. This was achieved by a commensurate increase in the number of documentaries, as well as a mounting number of variety and entertainment

PRICE SIXPENCE

programmes. The broadcasters' problem, and remember there were no commercial stations or alternatives to the BBC, was that they had evacuated most of their departments and it took a while for them to settle into their new rural environment outside of London.

Interestingly, these changes meant that the Home Programme was broadcasting for 17 hours each day, whereas before the war "a BBC day" lasted for just 14. On 1 November the first public appearance of BBC Symphony Orchestra at Bristol's Colston Hall was broadcast. Four days later there was the first broadcast of a complete Gilbert and Sullivan opera (*Trial by Jury*). Equally important as the reduction in records was the fact that there was less Sandy Macpherson at the theatre organ, and definitely

more "Variety". When war broke out he was giving up to three performances each day and had struggled to liven up proceedings. It was a question of who would succumb soonest – the audience from over exposure or Macpherson from exhaustion.

On Thursday 2 November, by no means an untypical evening, listening to the wireless would have provided a pretty mixed bag. Following the 6 o'clock news was a talk for the amateur handyman and then the first broadcast of an ENSA concert at an army camp "somewhere in England" featuring Jack Buchanan, Elsie Randolph, Fred Emney and Sid Millward and his Orchestra. ENSA (the Entertainment National Services Association) had been formed to specifically entertain the troops, and many

Vera Lynn singing for the forces in September 1940.

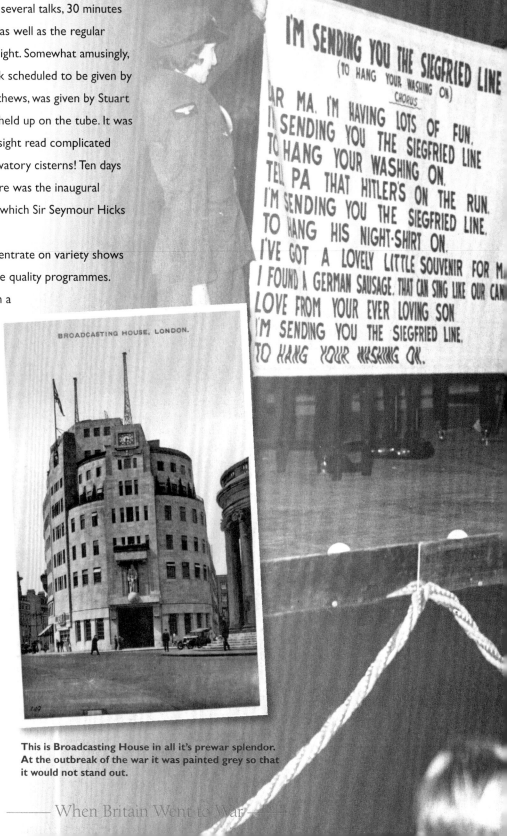

similar 30-minute programmes were featured on the radio throughout the war. Following ENSA there was an orchestral concert – one of several during the evening, and then an adaptation of A E W Mason's *The Four Feathers* – not inappropriate for wartime – several talks, 30 minutes of Government announcements as well as the regular news bulletins, at 9p.m. and midnight. Somewhat amusingly, on this particular evening the talk scheduled to be given by the amateur handyman, W R Mathews, was given by Stuart Hibberd since Mr Mathews was held up on the tube. It was no mean achievement having to sight read complicated instructions about maintaining lavatory cisterns! Ten days after the first ENSA concert there was the inaugural ENSA broadcast from France at which Sir Seymour Hicks was master of ceremonies.

The BBC did not simply concentrate on variety shows though, but was eager to produce quality programmes. This was ably demonstrated with a short series called *The Shadow of The Swastika*, in which they created dramatic reconstructions of the rise of the Nazi party. One letter-writer to the newspapers congratulated the BBC on their use of incidental music, saying it "suggested the cacophonies of what one of our poets has called 'the cohorts of the damned'". A 30-year-old actor named Marius Goring played the part of Hitler. In 1939 he had played the part of a U-boat captain in *The Spy in Black*; after the war he played a Nazi in *Ill-Met by Moonlight* as well as having a successful career in TV and films.

This is Broadcasting House in all it's prewar splendor. At the outbreak of the war it was painted grey so that it would not stand out.

When Britain Went to War

Adelaide Hall performing 'Hang out the Washing on the Siegfried Line' in October 1939.

A Royal Naval recruiting station in September 1939.

85

Christmas is Coming

From mid-November, with still little or no real war, a veritable jaw war developed, with Government ministers and their political opponents competing for media time. Amongst the ministers was Winston Churchill in his role as the First Lord of the Admiralty. In an upbeat speech reported by the *Mirror* he highlighted "how well the war has turned for the allies during the first 10 weeks". Prophetically, he spoke of the superior quality of the RAF against the Luftwaffe, and commented that the "mists and storms of winter" would act in Britain's favour. In a veiled comment he spoke of "a marked advantage in the higher range of science applied to war". He was of course referring to radar, which would be so important in the coming year.

"This is a queer war. First we had had four years of a peace that was anything but peaceful, now we had a war that, so far, was not nearly so warlike as we expected." **– Herbert Morrison, 27 November 1939**

On Monday 4 December, as 1939 drew to a close, the King visited the British Expeditionary Force in France. The British public was starved of any real information about his trip, and particularly any pictures, as the *Mirror* explained:

"This is the King in France with his troops. But all we can show you of him with his men are these three pictures of him landing at a French port. Why? Because Government officials are so bound up with red tape that they can't get a move on. The King can. He ORDERED on Monday that news of his presence in France should be made known immediately. Officialdom, he found out, would have withheld it until his return. You'd have thought that after that rebuff officialdom would have jumped to it yesterday. "But listen: Yesterday the King went to the Front Line; spent the day there. He lunched with the Guards; visited a hidden aerodrome. But we have no pictures – only these three of the Monday's landing in France. Photographs were taken of the King at the Front; they could have been flown to England in six hours... In time for this morning's papers. BUT THE GOVERNMENT CAN'T DO IT – IN SPITE OF THE KING'S COMMAND :'MY PEOPLE HAVE A RIGHT TO KNOW WHERE I AM.'"

This was all part of the ongoing issue of a government trying to get to grips with censorship, while at the same time attempting to wage a propaganda war. A week after

The *Graf Spee* scuppered following the battle of the River Plate.

the King's visit to France the BBC began a series of eight broadcasts entitled *The Voice of the Nazi* in which the Scotsman W A Sinclair discussed Nazi propaganda. In the second of these programmes, on Boxing Day 1939, Sinclair

talked about German radio's problems when discussing the sinking of the *Graf Spee*. On 15 December Germany had announced that their pocket battleship had won a famous victory – after which the truth came out, but the war had also moved on.

"Then, on the following days the Nazi announcements became hopelessly contradictory. First of all the German wireless said that the Graf Spee had soundly beaten three British cruisers, that she was undamaged, and had gone into Montevideo only because her food supply had been tainted by our alleged mustard-gas shells. Not long after, as you know, they had to admit that the ship was unseaworthy, and they then protested that she could not be repaired in the time allowed her by the Uruguayan Government. But the facts are common knowledge now, and the Nazis have had to admit that the Graf Spee has been scuttled and that her commander has committed suicide. This must have done more than any other single incident since the war began to arouse mistrust of the Nazi news in the ordinary German's mind." **– W A Sinclair, Voice of the Nazi, 26 December 1939**

Daily Mirror

No. 11,347 ◆ ONE PENNY

Registered at the G.P.O. as a Newspaper.

R.A.F. HERO'S ESCAPE

LOSING blood from a shot wound, a 14st. R.A.F. gunner, his plane's wings in tatters, was brought back safely by his plane's crew after he had shot down five Messerschmitts, crack German planes.

This story of the battle over Heligoland Bight, in which twelve German planes were brought down, was revealed last night.

The air gunner is now in hospital progressing favourably.

In the battle he was shot through the thigh, and the rest of the plane's crew all played their part in saving his life on the return journey.

Both wings of the plane were in tatters, and the fuselage was riddled with bullet holes. One wing had burst into flames, but the fire did not last long.

Carried from Plane

Despite the damage the aircraft "flew as well as ever." An armour-piercing bullet tore the sole from the boot of a member of the crew, but he escaped with a graze and a burn.

When the aircraft returned, the pilots and airmen made an escalator of their backs to remove the gunner from the machine.

The bullet which pierced his thigh missed both bone and artery, but he lost a great deal of blood on the long and extremely cold flight home.

Naval Honours

Officers and men of the submarine Spearfish have been honoured by the King for " courage, seamanship and resolution in bringing their ship safe home after many prolonged and violent enemy attacks which almost put her out of action."

These are the awards, announced last night:
Distinguished Service Cross: Lieutenant John Henry Eaden, R.N., commanding officer.
Distinguished Service Medal: Chief Engineroom Artificer Stanley N. Peel; Petty Officer Alfred P. Blackmore.

* These two men were specially commended by their commanding officer for their conduct.

Continued on Back Page

PETROL PRICE UP TO 1s. 10d.

THE price of petrol will be increased by a halfpenny from today, bringing it up to 1s. 10d. a gallon—the highest since February, 1924, when it was 1s. 11d.

Also from today the wholesale price of petrol in bulk to dealers and non-rebated commercial users will be 1s. 6½d. net.

Until further notice, commercial consumers who are currently paying full retail price, when calling at Petroleum Board depots for supplies into the tanks of their vehicles, will continue to be charged at retail price. All others calling at the depots will be charged a flat price of 1s. 8d. per gallon.

The charges, which have been agreed to by the Government, apply to deliveries in England, Wales and South Scotland. In other areas, such as the north of Scotland, the corresponding differentials will continue.

The Petroleum Board state that the object of the alterations has been to increase the dealer's retail margin.

The net return to the Petroleum Board will not be increased

More Pay

Wage increases which will cost the main line companies £1,000,000 a year have been granted to railwaymen.

The increase means a 50s. a week minimum for adults in traffic grades in London.

To All Our Readers This Christmastide We Say

BE STRONG AND OF GOOD CHEER

CHRISTMAS. AND AGAIN THE TIME HAS COME WHEN THE GREETING, " A MERRY CHRISTMAS " — THE WORDS MEN HAVE USED THROUGH THE CENTURIES — SEEMS FOR A MOMENT EMPTY OF MEANING.

Hitler has done his best to make this a sad Christmas. BUT HE HAS FAILED.

He has failed because in every way he underestimates the British people.

And if he thinks he is going to interfere with a British Christmas—that is just another mistake he has made.

✦ ✦ ✦

True, the youth of the Empire is scattered in war; many children wisely evacuated to new and safer homes.

Around the firesides there will be reunions; but there will be many who will be there only in thought.

The pictures in the fire will be of absent men and women —on guard for Britain: doing their job.

We will have visions of them all.

At sea the Navy and Merchant Navy keeping their ceaseless watch in mine - strewn waters, heroes every hour.

On land the troops facing the German lines, the anti-aircraft men at their posts.

In the air, the flyers maintaining their tireless vigil in the clouds.

We shall think of them.

✦ ✦ ✦

And let us remember also those who have made the great sacrifice, and their saddened homes.

Those sacrifices can never have been made in vain if we all play our part, resolute and determined to see this thing through until truth and right and liberty are established once again.

So this Christmas of 1939 let there be a smile on your lips, and in your heart confidence.

✦ ✦ ✦

And next Christmas !

Well, that is looking a long way ahead.

Remember the tasks that lie ahead of us.

But down the coming year we will march on in our own British way—to sure and certain triumph over evil.

Then the next Christmas can be a real riotous merry one.

FLYING ATLANTIC TO ATTEND PARTY

SIX-YEAR-OLD Helen Halford and her brother, John, who is four, children of an R.A.F. pilot, are to fly the Atlantic to attend a party.

They will board the transatlantic Clipper on Christmas Day and two days later they will be at their home in Broughton, near Stockbridge, Hants.

Mrs. Halford, their mother, told the *Daily Mirror* last night: " It will probably be a thrill for them—it will certainly be a great thrill for us.

" They went over in the Queen Mary to stay with my sister in New York when war began.

" A nurse will accompany them on the flight.

" I'm flying to Paris beforehand, and I'll be at Lisbon to greet them as they step from the plane.

" We are going to give them a party when they get home. It is a pity they won't be here for Christmas, but they couldn't get seats on the Christmas plane.

" I don't know whether they will bring Christmas presents for us—I should hardly think so, for luggage must be so light on the Clipper.

" Their best Christmas gift, and ours, too, will be our being together again."

The War's First Christmas

As the Mirror noted on its front page on 23 December, "Hitler has done his best to make this a sad Christmas. BUT HE HAS FAILED." There was an effort to adopt a confident tone and to even suggest that Christmas 1940 would be a better one, with the war perhaps even over.

The rest of the news was an odd mixture of German raiders being shot down, servicemen getting married, reports on German propaganda speeches by Dr Goebbels, and even a new series, "Our Court of Sex Appeal".

What Is sex appeal? In general, it is that elusive something which attracts a man to a woman, or a woman to a man. Its basis is physical. Yet sex appeal is not entirely dependent upon "body-urge". For instance, a plain woman or an ugly man may prove irresistibly attractive, while a person of outstanding beauty may remain unloved and unlovable.

Some of the great lovers of history have been far from beautiful. Cleopatra was thin and plain; Mirabeau was pockmarked and hideous. So sex appeal is not mere beauty.

Then, is sex appeal wit, or brain? Again, no. Some of the most stupid women in the world have tremendous sex appeal. You see, therefore, that this quality is hard to define. Yet one recognises it when one sees it.

And so we have formed the COURT OF SEX APPEAL.

Even advertisers found a way of working the war, Christmas and staying healthy into their pitch.

Readers of the Daily Mirror, whether male or female, are invited to fill in the form below, and to post it to us with a photograph attached. The most interesting cases will be chosen for a special session of the Court.

*Your details and picture will then be placed before the Court, and judged — according to combined standards of beauty, cleverness and personality. **You** will be examined for general attractiveness — SEX APPEAL.*

If you are chosen, the details which you give on the form on this page will be discussed frankly by the Judge, the Counsel for the Defence and the Counsel for the Prosecution,

And the Jury will decide your rating in sex appeal.

1940
Invasion?

After months of "Phoney War", spring heralded the coming of real war. For much of the winter the propaganda war orchestrated by Lord Haw-Haw both annoyed and fascinated people. The war of words extended to some political infighting within the Government, leading to the resignation of Neville Chamberlain and the coming to power of Winston Churchill just in time for the almost disastrous retreat from Dunkirk. All too soon the Battle of Britain was to begin and the war would arrive on the home front. The question on everyone's mind was "will we be invaded?".

"Perhaps it will come tonight, Perhaps it will come next week, Perhaps it will never come… we shall seek no terms, we shall tolerate no parley – we may show mercy – we shall ask for none." **– Winston Churchill, 14 July 1940**

A downed Heinkel 111 'somewhere in Scotland'.

1 January • More men called up in Britain
1 February • Russians launch major offensive against Finland
12 March • Treaty signed ending Russian war in Finland
16 March • Luftwaffe attacks Royal Navy fleet in Scapa Flow
6 April • Allied troops begin laying mines in Norwegian waters
9 April • Germany invades Denmark and Norway
14 April • Allied troops land in Narvik, Norway
2 May • Allied troops begin evacuation for Norway
10 May • Germany invades the Low Countries
• Chamberlain resigns as PM to be replaced by Winston Churchill
12 May • Germany begins advance into France
14 May • The launch of Local Defence Volunteers (renamed the Home Guard in July)
15 May • The Netherlands surrenders
17 May • Brussels is captured
22 May • Britain breaks Germany's Enigma code
26 May • Evacuation from Dunkirk begins
28 May • Belgium surrenders
3 June • Last troops leave Dunkirk
8 June • Norway falls
10 June • Italy declares war on the Allies
11 June • Italian planes bomb Malta
14 June • Germans enter Paris
22 June • France signs armistice with Germany
19 July • Battle of Britain begins
13 August • Eagle Day, the launch of Goering's offensive to gain control of the skies over Britain
17 August • Hitler announces a total blockade of Britain
25 August • RAF bombs Berlin in a night raid

Troops evacuated from Dunkirk on their way through Kent getting some much needed refreshments.

A New Year's War

On New Year's Day 1940 Britain awoke to the news that the Finnish Army had routed the Russians after a two-day battle on the frozen Lake Kianta. For many this seemed like a war being fought elsewhere: British soldiers and airmen were not often involved, with the exception of th Navy, which was protecting lifeline convoys.

But later on New Year's Day the war was brought that bit closer to millions of British homes when it was announced that nearly two million men, aged 19 to 27 years old, were to be called up. Men who had reached the age of 28 by 1 January 1940 were excluded. This meant that the number of men called to arms was to be over 3 million.

Just to prove that life continued on the home front there was a report on the front page of the *Daily Mirror* about a whistle blower and his wife.

"Because a wife started throwing cups and saucers at her husband, who blew a whistle, hundreds of people were roused from their beds in the belief that an air raid was about to start. Edward Wilson – the target for utensils – of East Lane, Bluetown, Sheemess, described at Sheerness Police Court yesterday how all the trouble started when he appeared on a charge of unlawfully creating a noise by blowing a whistle without cause. He pleaded guilty and told the Court he had taken his children to a party. When he returned home his 'missus' started throwing cups and saucers at him. 'So,' said Wilson, 'I knocked her down. What else could I do then but to blow the police whistle for help?' The whistle, Police Constable Pryke told the Court, resulted in a number of people rushing in all directions. Inspector Young

Men being examined at a recruitment centre in Kingston-upon-Thames.

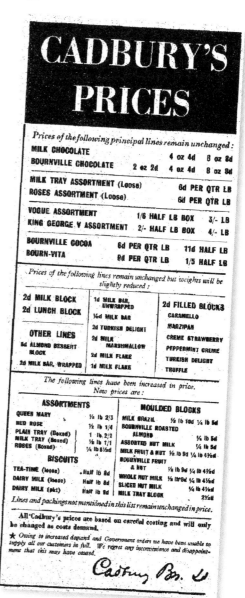

BLACK OUT 4.29 p.m. TILL 7.38 a.m.

During the depths of winter the black-out was long; times were carried on the *Daily Mirror's* back page every day.

said: 'The whistle caused consternation, not only in Bluetown, but in Miletown, about two miles away. It was aggravated by the fact that notice had recently been given notifying the public that whistles would be blown to warn them of air raids.' Fining Wilson £1, the chairman, Mr W N Rule, said the Bench assumed that he had acted in ignorance, 'but it is a serious matter'."

The need for the call up of even more men was underlined 10 days later when a German Messerschmitt ME-108, lost in fog, crashed in Belgium, near Mechelen-

sur-Meuse. On board were two officers who were carrying plans for the German offensive against Belgium and Holland, which showed it was slated to begin on 17 January. The capture of the two men, and the papers they did not manage to burn, led to Hitler postponing the offensive. General Gamelin, commander-in-chief of the French Army and the Allied commander-in-chief thought the whole thing was a trick! In any event, the discovery resulted in all leave being cancelled and troops and the RAF being placed on full alert.

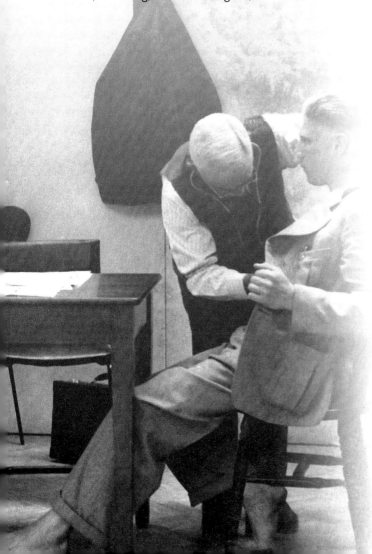

Shortages of supply affected the price of chocolate, although Cadbury's suggested that prices should remain the same on some items, with just the weight going down!

Radio Haw-Haw

For both the BBC and the newspapers one of their biggest challenges was dealing with the flow of news, and sometimes the lack of it, from the Ministry of Information. The Ministry were anxious to ensure, not unreasonably, that all sections of the media told the public a version of what was happening that met with their approval. However, the absurdity of the situation regarding the release of information was highlighted on 5 January when the Minister for War, Leslie Hore-Belisha, resigned and the news was broadcast first by German radio. Naturally, with their print deadlines newspapers were not best placed to carry up-to-the-minute news; however, the BBC should not have been so hampered.

As the *Daily Mirror* reported the following day, "Actually, he has been dismissed because the generals objected to his reforms and made representations to the premier. Hore-Belisha knew nothing of his fate until Mr Chamberlain called him into conference yesterday. He was amazed and unhesitatingly refused the new post offered to him."

It was episodes like this that added to the feeling among many people in Britain that Germany somehow had the inside track on what was happening in the corridors of power, as well as on the streets of Britain. As early as 27 October 1939 the *Daily Mirror* received a letter from a Mrs Turner of Isis Street, London, SW16:

"The BBC is entitled to its 10 shillings, if only to hear Lord Haw-Haw from Hamburg announcing for Adolph and his pals. His lordship seems to think he's taking their part! Haw-Haw gives even old women like me a good laugh, as I take all his talks the other way round."

Lord Haw-Haw has today become something of a joke figure, but despite comments like those of Mrs Turner there were signs at the time that some people regarded him very differently. A BBC memorandum a month later stated: "Recent investigation has shown that a vast and increasing number of listeners is tuning in regularly to the 'Lord Haw-Haw' broadcasts from Germany. To begin with, listeners took these as entertainment, and laughed heartily at them, but indications are growing that they are being taken seriously by a good many listeners, especially women."

Such was the Haw-Haw effect that increasingly many people believed that Germany was winning the propaganda war. While 16 million people in Britain usually listened to the 9pm BBC News, around 6 million switched over to Hamburg to catch Haw-Haw at 9.15pm.

Initially Lord Haw-Haw was in fact the nick-name given to Wolf Mittler, a German national who had been educated in Britain and spoke with an exaggerated upper-class British accent; "Haw-Haw" had its origins in the mid 19th century, used to describe someone with just such a speech pattern as Mittler's.

By January stories like the one about the Boy Scouts were increasingly being featured and picked up by the paper to try to show the absurdity of the Haw-Haw menace. By this time, William Joyce, the man whom we now think of as Lord Haw-Haw, had taken over from Mittler. The man who made the phrase "Jairmany Calling" his trademark has been called "one of the twentieth century's most notorious voices". It's hard to disagree. Many also found the Irishman one of the most irritating; he had an innate ability to sound authoritarian, smug and hectoring – all in the same sentence.

It's the Boy Scouts Now!

Silence for Lord Haw-Haw. . . . This is what he had to say last night about sabotage in Yugoslavia:—

"Groups of British Boy Scouts have been frequently observed camping in those places where afterwards acts of sabotage have occurred and where factories have been burned down.

Daily Mirror

No. 11,257   ONE PENNY

Registered at the G.P.O. as a Newspaper.

BELISHA RESIGNS

Stanley Is War Chief

Dispute With Generals

Mr. Hore-Belisha . . . leaves the War Office and goes out of the Government.

A SENSATIONAL CHANGE IN THE WAR CABINET WAS ANNOUNCED LAST NIGHT. MR. LESLIE HORE-BELISHA, THE MAN RESPONSIBLE FOR PURGING THE ARMY COUNCIL OF ITS OLD MEN, HAS RESIGNED THE OFFICE OF WAR MINISTER. ACTUALLY, HE HAS BEEN DISMISSED BECAUSE THE GENERALS OBJECTED TO HIS REFORMS AND MADE REPRESENTATIONS TO THE PREMIER.

Hore-Belisha knew nothing of his fate until Mr. Chamberlain called him into conference yesterday. He was amazed and unhesitatingly refused the new post offered to him.

He is succeeded by Mr. Oliver Stanley, whose chief claim to fame is that he is a son of Lord Derby, himself a War Minister in the last war.

Lord Macmillan, the Minister of Information, has also resigned. The new Minister is Sir John Reith, famous first head of the B.B.C.

Sir Andrew Duncan, a leader of the iron and steel industry, becomes the new President of the Board of Trade, in succession to Mr. Stanley.

Neither Sir Andrew nor Sir John is at present in Parliament. Seats will probably be found for them.

The announcement of sensational Ministerial changes, made late last night, will stagger M.P.s of all parties, writes the "Daily Mirror" Diplomatic Correspondent. There had been no hint of differences in the Government.

The Ministry of Information, of course, has always been a weak spot in the Chamberlain administration, and Lord Macmillan's departure is scarcely surprising.

Revolt by Generals

But the resignation of the War Minister, at this stage in the war, is the biggest political sensation since hostilities began.

Despite the denials of policy differences in the letters that have passed between Mr. Hore-Belisha and the Premier, it is obvious that a War Minister does not resign unless he has been repudiated by his chief on a major issue.

It was, in fact, a revolt by the generals. Hore-Belisha's "live wire" methods, his demand for a democratic Army has roused the opposition of the military caste—the old gang of the Army Command.

The old gang took their case to the Premier, and Mr. Chamberlain, anxious to appease the generals, decided to sack his War Minister. It is the first victory of the generals.

Big Following

The Prime Minister offered Mr. Hore-Belisha another Ministerial post—almost certainly the Presidency of the Board of Trade, now vacated by Mr. Stanley.

Belisha refused, he could scarcely have accepted.

The ex-War Minister has a big following in the House.

Continued on Back Page

Mr. Oliver Stanley moves from the Board of Trade to take Mr. Hore-Belisha's place.

FINNS GET OUR BEST

BRITAIN is sending to Finland equipment and clothing originally intended for the British Army.

Besides helping Finland, Britain is sending arms and munitions to help Sweden's re-armament, it was announced in London last night.

Although Sweden is helping Finland, the arms and munitions sent to Sweden are for her own use.

Meanwhile the expansion of the British Army goes on and Britain's own war effort is still gathering speed.

While no details of voluntary recruitment can be published, it can be stated that the first hundred thousand has been easily passed.

National service has changed the whole character of the Army, it was stated. It has "completely democratised" the forces.

M. Paul Naggiar, French Ambassador to Soviet Russia, was reported last night to be following Sir William Seeds, the British Ambassador, from Moscow.

Sir William Seeds left on Tuesday, and the following day Signor Rosso, Italian Ambassador, left.

"DISSENSION IN ENEMY CAMP"

German political quarters welcomed the report of Mr. Hore-Belisha's resignation as an indication of possible dissensions in the enemy camp, and, secondly, because Mr Hore-Belisha is Jewish.

Foreign and unofficial suggestions that the resignation might portend peace overtures were considered unlikely by well-informed Nazis in view of other developments, particularly the alleged British intention to extend the theatre of war to Scandinavia.—British United Press.

MR. OLIVER STANLEY ILL

Mr. Oliver Stanley, the new War Minister, was unable to attend the conference of the Federation of University Conservative and Unionist Associations yesterday, owing to illness.

He is in bed at his London home with a slight chill, but hopes to return to his duties in a day or two.

Sir Oswald Mosley (second left with moustache) among his fascists in Newcastle in July 1934; a meeting likely to have been attended by William Joyce.

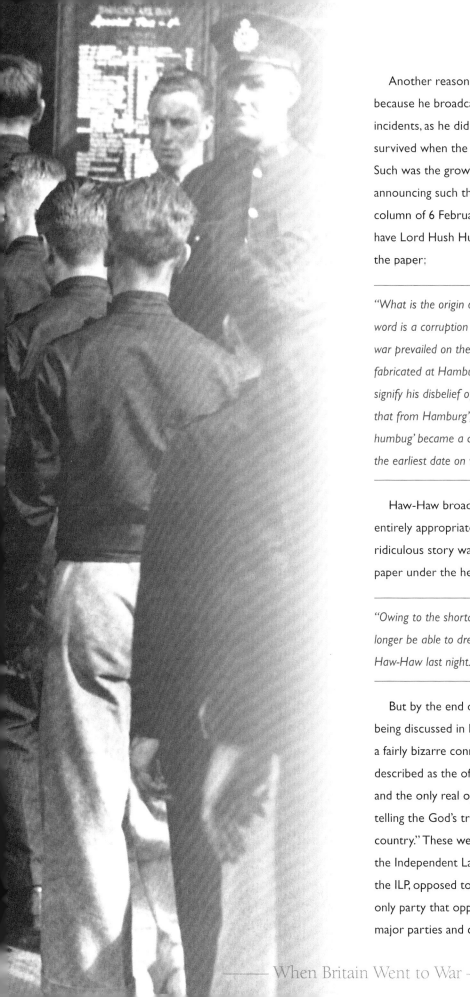

Another reason that people listened to Haw-Haw was because he broadcast the names of survivors from naval incidents, as he did on 2 February 1940 after 30 seamen survived when the submarine HMS *Undine* was lost. Such was the growing resentment over Lord Haw-Haw announcing such things that the *Daily Mirror* in its leader column of 6 February said: "Instead of Lord Haw-Haw we have Lord Hush Hush." A few days later came this piece in the paper:

"What is the origin of the term 'humbug'? This frequently used word is a corruption of Hamburg. During the period when war prevailed on the Continent so many false reports were fabricated at Hamburg that at length, when anyone would signify his disbelief of a statement, he would say: 'You had that from Hamburg', and hence 'That is Hamburg' or 'That Is humbug' became a common expression of incredulity. 1785 is the earliest date on which this word appeared in print."

Haw-Haw broadcast from Hamburg, and so it seemed entirely appropriate, when, in February 1940, this ridiculous story was broadcast and lampooned in the paper under the headline "SO WE SHOULD HOPE".

"Owing to the shortage of oils in England, housewives will no longer be able to dress their salads with cod liver oil," said Lord Haw-Haw last night.

But by the end of February Lord Haw-Haw was even being discussed in Parliament, although it has to be said in a fairly bizarre connection. "I have heard Lord Haw-Haw described as the official opposition to the Government and the only real opposition in the country. That man's telling the God's truth about the old people of this country." These were the words of John McGovern MP of the Independent Labour Party for Glasgow Shettleston; the ILP, opposed to the war on ethical grounds, was the only party that opposed the wartime truce between the major parties and contested elections.

The Man behind Lord Haw-Haw

Joyce was born in April 1906 in New York to an English mother and an Irish father. He moved with his family to Ireland three years later, growing up in County Mayo. The family moved to England when Joyce was 15 and two years later he was demonstrating strongly anti-Semitic views, although he was far from alone in Britain in this. Having joined the Conservative Party, by 1932 Joyce was almost inevitably drawn to Sir Oswald Moseley's British Union of Fascists. But in contrast to Moseley, who had a relaxed – some said an almost charming manner – Joyce was by all accounts a nasty, angry man. By 1937 Joyce had split from the BUF and formed his own party – the British National Socialist League. A week before war broke out Joyce, together with his family, fled to Berlin after a tip-off that his arrest was imminent.

In Berlin he quickly ingratiated himself with the German Foreign Ministry, leading to a job on German radio. "Jairmany Calling" seemed to reveal details that only a man with a network of spies and informers could possibly know, and proved perversely attractive to listeners starved of what they saw as real information from the BBC who, to be fair, were merely doing as much as the Ministry of Information allowed them.

"Rumours attributing to the German wireless an intimate knowledge of British local events through secret channels are without foundation, states the Ministry of Information. It is clearly important that no individual should help to undermine confidence by repeating these rumours at all events unless he has personally tuned in to Germany and heard the statement for himself. If Germans possessed secret channels in British towns for obtaining such information they would scarcely be likely to advertise the fact. On some occasions there may be a perfectly simple explanation of German broadcast descriptions of local events in Britain."

Quite apart from the slightly odd notion that it was only men who tuned into German radio there is an inference that things were only untrue if they were repeated!

By March 1940 Haw-Haw's identity was finally exposed as the 35-year-old Joyce. The *Daily Mirror* revealed that he had been known as "the Professor" during his BUP days and, after he had his face slashed with a razor, as "Scarface Joyce". In the true spirit of investigative journalism the *Daily Mirror* tracked down the mother of Joyce's wife, who was with him in Germany. She was in fact his second wife. The article went on to describe her in some detail:

Margot White's mother, although she does not admit that Lord Haw-Haw is her son-in-law, told the Daily Mirror yesterday that her daughter married William Joyce, the former official of Mosley's party who has been identified as the German propagandist by his first wife, who lives in Glasgow. Joyce's first marriage was dissolved, and shortly afterwards he married Margot.

They went to the Continent for a honeymoon trip "just before the war started", Mrs White said. "We can only assume that they are in Germany, because we have not heard anything from Margot." Margot, who is 28, joined the Mosley party, but disagreed with its leader, and along with Joyce and a number of other officials she was dismissed. She was fond of social life and dancing, and was nearly always to be seen smoking cigarettes through a long holder. When Margot White joined the Carlisle branch of the Fascists she became one of its most prominent members.

Meet Lady Haw-Haw, wife of the hypo-critical "Hamburger." Hers is the voice you hear every night announcing the programme.
Picture above shows her as a ballet dancer and (below) a studio portrait.

TELLS ON RADIO OF GAY NAZI LIFE

THE mysterious woman who broadcasts on the Hamburg radio, and has become known as "Lady Haw-Haw," is, in fact, entitled to that name, for she is the second wife of the man who, during the past six months, has made for himself the most outstanding name in broadcasting.

Lady Haw-Haw was before her marriage two years ago Miss Margaret White, known to her friends as Margot. She is the daughter of Mr. and Mrs. E. R. White, who now live at Bellott-street, Cheetham Hill, Manchester.

Lady Haw-Haw has several times

Contd. on Back Page, Col. 4

SHIP SUNK: 68 SAVED

Seventeen European and fifty-one Lascar members of the crew of the Harrison Line steamer Counsellor (5,068 tons), of Liverpool, were landed at a north-west coast port yesterday after their vessel had been sunk by an explosion.

Having found out Haw-Haw's real identity, his effectiveness seemed to diminish, with far fewer references in the newspapers to his preposterous claims. By late March 1940 and the Easter holiday, record crowds were being reported at holiday resorts. Cars on the road to Bournemouth averaged 1,400 per hour.

At the end of March the BBC's German service introduced their own "Lord Haw-Haw", Karl Stepanek, a Czech actor who had been very popular in Germany before the war. He told the *Daily Mirror*, "I did not come here to earn a living or to be in safety. I came to take my share in the fight against Germany and to win back the freedom of my people."

After the Battle of Britain and the start of the war on the Eastern front Haw-Haw's collateral went even further downhill – although he still occasionally hit the mark. Joyce took German citizenship, which failed to stop him from being tried in Britain for treason – the fact that he was born in America and was more Irish than English did nothing to help him either. Joyce was executed in January 1946.

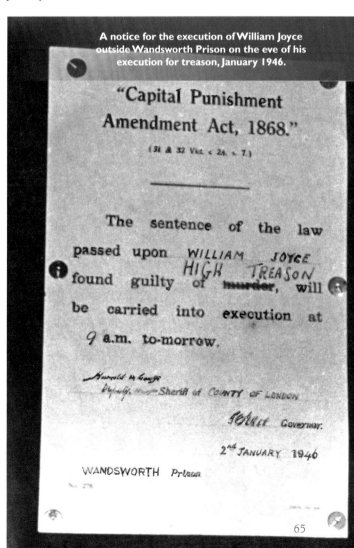

A notice for the execution of William Joyce outside Wandsworth Prison on the eve of his execution for treason, January 1946.

The Big Freeze

During January 1940 Britain suffered its coldest weather in 100 years – so cold that the sea froze. Not that this dominated the news, since the censors had banned any mention of it until after it had passed. Near Bognor Regis ice stretched for 300 yards along the shore. A woman found dead in her bath in Islington, London, was sitting in a block of ice.

Just how this was going to be helpful to the Germans is unclear, as the whole of Europe had been covered in deep snow as Arctic air blew down from Siberia. In Buxton in Derbyshire temperatures dropped to 33 below zero, in London to 25 degrees below.

The Thames froze over at Kingston and for eight

A milkman delivering milk on 18 January.

miles between Teddington and Sunbury; there was a foot of ice on London's reservoirs. The cold followed some exceptionally foggy weather that kept the Channel Islands' steamer at sea for three days with 200 passengers on board.

The number of deaths from the weather was unknown, but more people were injured from exploding kitchen boilers than were injured on the western front. A family of six died in Newcastle after lighting a fire beneath their empty kitchen boiler.

The Thames at Kingston, Surrey.

A War of Words

By the end of January the Government's handling of the flow of information was continuing to receive criticism; neither was its conduct of the war effort receiving universal approval. On 27 January Winston Churchill spoke to a crowd of 2,500 at a meeting in Manchester's Free Trade Hall. Just before he spoke a heckler was heard shouting, "We want Mosley!" On being asked if he wanted the man thrown out, Churchill said "No, let me deal with him, I've had 40 years' experience of this kind of thing." In his speech he urged people not to become downhearted at the shipping losses and suggested that half the German Navy's submarines had been destroyed – a claim that was later met with derision by the Nazi media. According to the *Daily Mirror*, Churchill was "the No.1 star of the Government's feeble enough radio team", and despite a characteristic speech there was little or no clapping when he suggested, "the passive war policy of the

Government was right". It was, as we now know with hindsight, the lull before the storm; and in Britain, with continuing shortages and a feeling of the hatches being battened down, pressure was building up. People wanted a release.

In the same issue as Churchill's speech there was a picture and short report about the man Hitler had chosen to "rule Britain" after the invasion. Wilhelm Bohle, the Nazi *gauleiter* born in Bradford in 1904 was the man. The *Daily Mirror* probably judged the nation's mood to perfection, saying "Hitler has chosen the man who will rule Britain for him after he has put us to sleep for a fortnight and meanwhile occupied the country."

In its leader column the paper made sure that its readers were in no doubt where the paper stood on the issue of fighting the good fight. It raised Churchill's speech, saying that everyone should learn by heart its closing sentences. Today this particular speech has been overshadowed by many of the other remarkable speeches that Churchill would later give. But it is one of the earliest examples of his wartime rhetoric that has the undeniable stamp of greatness.

"Come then, let us to the task, to the battle and the toil – Each to our part, each to our station. Fill the armies, rule the air, pour out the munitions. Strangle the U-boats, sweep the mines. Plough the land, build the ships. Guard the streets, succour the wounded. Uplift the downcast and honour the brave."

Winston Churchill was beginning to get into his stride. The *Daily Mirror* was very supportive of the First Lord of the Admiralty, particularly as the paper became more disillusioned with Chamberlain.

Humour was also a powerful weapon in the fight, although there's less to make one laugh about in this particular

"Though thou shouldest make thy nest as high as the eagle, I will bring thee down from thence, saith the Lord." Jeremiah 49. 16.

Text for the Eagle of Berchtesgaden!

cartoon than many. It has a sense of irony about it now, but also a sure sense of resisting the Nazi menace.

Three weeks after Churchill made his speech in Manchester, just before 4am on 18 February, the Destroyer HMS *Daring* was torpedoed and sunk off the Pentland Firth by a German U-boat; just five of the crew of 162 survived. The Ministry of Information was keen to suppress news of the disaster, especially given that it was the sixth destroyer to have been lost since the war began – the Admiralty delayed announcing the news until the following morning and the BBC duly reported it in their news bulletin. It was not until the 20th that newspapers caught up with events.

The incident brought to a head the media's relationship with the Ministry. While everyone agreed it was important to leave out distressing detail such as "sunk in one minute", it was important to be factual and not have the German media steal a march. A month later the fiasco surrounding British reporting of the German raid on Scapa Flow galvanized the Government into action.

On the evening of 16 March German aircraft attacked Scapa Flow and inflicted some minor damage on the base. The Admiralty asked the BBC not to broadcast news of the raid, despite the fact that BBC monitors had heard a German broadcast during the night provide details of the attack. By mid-morning French radio had broadcast a statement issued by the German High Command, and it was only on the 1 o'clock news that an Admiralty statement was finally broadcast. Naturally, the newspapers were a day behind, but the *Mirror* decided to capitalize on the story of the first civilian death during an air raid. However, it was not the newspaper's main headline: that was reserved for the meeting between Mussolini and Hitler.

In his diary entry for 27 March, Sir John Reith, then Minister of Information, noted that the Prime Minister said: "We weren't taking propaganda seriously enough in this country." Chamberlain also told his Minister of Information that he thought the war was going to go on "more or less indefinitely as it is now". Staggering as it may now seem, Reith was not part of the Cabinet – this fact alone meant that Britain was trailing in Germany's wake in the propaganda war.

Place Your Regular Order Today!

No. 1,307

TWOPENCE

Sunday Pictorial

Churchill's 3 Warnings to the Nation

GILMOUR DIES— THE SADDEST MAN IN THE CABINET!

See Page 4

MR. WINSTON CHURCHILL, broadcasting last night, gave three warnings to the nation:

1 " AN INTENSIFICATION OF THE WAR IS TO BE EXPECTED."

2 " I CANNOT ASSURE YOU THAT THE WAR WILL BE SHORT, STILL LESS THAT IT WILL BE EASY."

3 " UP TO THE PRESENT, TIME HAS BEEN ON OUR SIDE; BUT TIME IS A CHANGEABLE ALLY."

" It is no part of our policy to seek a war with Russia," said Mr. Churchill.

It was a speech ending a week which has heartened the Allies more than the Nazis.

Mr. Churchill's inspiring words went, as well as to the whole of Britain, to the Forces, the Empire and the U.S.A.

Mr. Churchill said:—

" Up to the present, Time has been on our side, but Time is a changeable ally.

" IT SEEMS TO ME THAT AN INTENSIFICATION OF THE STRUGGLE IS TO BE EXPECTED, AND WE ARE CERTAINLY BY NO MEANS INCLINED TO SHRINK FROM IT.

" We do not conceal from ourselves that trials and tribulations lie before us far beyond anything we have so far undergone; and we know that supreme exertions will be required from the British and French nations. But we are entitled to recognise the basic facts.

" Our resources and our manpower, once they are fully developed, massively exceed those of the enemy.

♦ ♦ ♦

" People often ask me, WILL THE WAR BE LONG OR SHORT?

" It might have been a very short war—perhaps indeed there might have been no war—if all the neutral states who share our convictions upon fundamental matters, and openly or secretly sympathise with us, had stood together at one signal and in one line.

" We did not count on this, and therefore we are not dismayed.

" I cannot assure you that the war will be short, and still less that it will be easy.

" But it would not be right, or in the general interest, that the weak-

ness of neutrals should feed the Aggressor's strength and fill to overflowing the cup of human woe.

" In his frenzy, this wicked man and the criminal regime which he has conceived and erected, increasingly turn their malice upon the weak, the lonely and above all the unarmed vessels of countries with which Germany is still supposed to be in friendly relations.

" During the last fortnight fourteen neutral ships have been sunk, and only one British ship." Mr. Churchill repeated, "—only one British ship ! After all, it is we who are his foes.

" Why, only yesterday, while the sailors from a British submarine were carrying ashore on stretchers eight emaciated Dutchmen whom they had rescued from six days' exposure in an open boat, Dutch aviators, in the name of strict and impartial orthodoxy, were shooting down a British aircraft which had lost its way.

[*The story of these men's sufferings is on page 3.*]

" We shall follow this war wherever it leads us; but we have no wish to broaden the area of conflict.

" IT IS NO PART OF OUR POLICY TO SEEK A WAR WITH RUSSIA.

" Our affair is with Hitler and the Nazi-German power."

Mr. Churchill's final words were withering:

" MORE THAN A MILLION GERMAN SOLDIERS, INCLUDING NEARLY ALL THEIR ACTIVE DIVISIONS, AND ARMOURED DIVISIONS, ARE DRAWN UP READY TO STRIKE AT A FEW HOURS' NOTICE ALL ALONG THE FRONTIERS OF LUXEMBOURG, BELGIUM AND HOLLAND.

" And the decision rests in the hands of a haunted, morbid being who, to their eternal shame, the German peoples in their bewilderment have worshipped as a god."

a good week!

THE LADY ON THE LEFT IS HAPPY—SMILING. AND THAT IS WHY HER FACE APPEARS ON OUR FRONT PAGE TODAY.

THERE'S A WAR ON. HARSH CRITICISM IS OFTEN A DUTY.

BUT REMEMBER — LONG FACES WON'T WIN A WAR. AND NOBODY WILL QUESTION THE GOVERNMENT'S WISDOM IN ASKING US ALL TO REMAIN CHEERFUL !

★

BESIDES—THIS HAS BEEN A GOOD WEEK FOR BRITAIN AND FRANCE.

" Today we applaud the Government," says our leading article on page fourteen.

This has been a week of action, and Reynaud's arrival at the head of the French Government has encouraged the Allies to take the initiative in several fields.

★

WHY SHOULDN'T WE BE CHEERFUL, ANYWAY ?

Haven't you seen the crocuses in full bloom ? Haven't you noticed that the daffodils are nearly bursting their buds ? Can't you feel the difference in the air —that wine-like exhilaration which betokens the Spring ?

★

We've a lot to be thankful for. Let's all look on the bright side—remember that " Your merry heart goes all the way "— and it's much better travelling !

DON'T LET THEM FOOL YOU ABOUT RUSSIA! SEE PAGE TWO

War Arrives on the Western Front

By the end of March, with better weather in Europe it was inevitable that fighting would become a reality. In the middle of the month the War Cabinet had been told that the Germans were planning an attack on Holland, giving rise to concerns about the weakness of the BEF in France. Then, on 26 March, word was received from the British Air Attaché in Sweden that the Germans were about to mount an attack on Norway. It was against this background that Winston Churchill gave the fifth of his wartime broadcasts to the nation, one that made quite clear what Britain could expect. The end of "the Bore War" was just around the corner.

In his speech Churchill spoke of it being "all quiet on the western front" where over a million men of the German Army ranged along the frontier with France and the neutral countries; it was just a matter of time before there was an attack. Ten days later Germany acted and attacked Norway. On 9 April Oslo Radio announced that German troops had disembarked at Egersund on the south coast of Norway and that Kristiansand had been attacked. Lord Haw-Haw reported "No significant resistance was offered along the coast of Norway except near Oslo. Resistance there was broken during the afternoon and Oslo itself was occupied." Yet German radio's boast of "no significant resistance" in Norway was not entirely true. Germany's newest cruiser, the *Bluecher*, was sunk by the 55-year-old guns of Oslo's coastal fort; around 1,000 men, mostly soldiers, lost their lives. The pocket battleship *Lutzow* was also damaged.

Two days before the invasion of Norway a British naval task force had sailed from Scapa Flow to mine the waters off the coast of Norway. One of the ships, the destroyer HMS *Glowworm*, became detached from the main fleet during a violent storm and was spotted by a German destroyer and the *Admiral Hipper*, a cruiser. Badly damaged by the cruiser's guns and unable to outrun it, the *Glowworm*'s captain, Lieutenant-Commander Roope, fired 10 torpedoes but scored no hits and so the destroyer was soon set on fire. Roope successfully rammed the cruiser before firing one more salvo, scoring a hit. The *Glowworm* sank with the loss of 118 men; there were only 31 survivors. The *Admiral Hipper* picked up the survivors, but Roope was drowned. The captain of the *Admiral Hipper* wrote to the International Red Cross recommending Roope be given a medal for his bravery. Accordingly, he was awarded the VC; this was the first to be awarded in the Second World War, although awarded posthumously, in July 1945.

None of this was reported at the time. It was not until May 1945 that the story of the ramming appeared in the *Daily Mirror* when one of the crew was repatriated from Italy having been a POW for the duration. In July 1945 when Lieutenant-Commander Roope was awarded his VC the *Daily Mirror* reported what chief petty officer Jack Townsley, who had just returned to Portland, told the paper. Townsley was sitting on the fast-sinking keel of the *Glowworm* after the battle, with Lieutenant-Commander Roope, who turned to him and said: "Well, Townsley, I don't suppose we shall ever play cricket again." Such were the logistical difficulties of news-gathering that many incidents were reported only as a matter of luck.

Despite some stout Norwegian defence in some areas, particularly around Oslo, the result of the invasion was a foregone conclusion. South Norway eventually fell around the beginning of May, and on 7 June 1940 King Haakon and his Government left Norway on board HMS *Devonshire*. In Denmark the King ordered his troops not to resist, against overwhelming German odds, and the country capitulated immediately – the war on the western front had begun.

I-Spy Spies

Less than two weeks after war broke out the *Daily Mirror* warned its readers about the dangers of spies. It reported a notice that had appeared in all pubs in the Aldershot area, home to many army units. "Warning! Walls have ears. Information, which might be of great value to the enemy, is being discussed in hotels, public houses, bars and general meeting places. The enemy spy system is extensive and a chance remark made in complete innocence may have

disastrous effects." It also carried a warning of "severe penalties" for men with the colours discussing military matters. This was the start of a national obsession with spies and spying that steadily grew throughout the early months of the war and reached something of a crescendo as real fighting on the western front led people to believe an invasion was not just a figment of the Führer's imagination.

A week later an unnamed man broadcast on the BBC, calling himself E7 suggested that "Unguarded words may help the enemy, so keep a finger on your lip." He went on

to say that he "had no intention of starting a spy scare".
He probably didn't start it and scare may be too strong a
word, but his broadcast fanned the flames. The release of
a film starring Edward G Robinson called *Confessions of a
Nazi Spy* only added to such fears – despite its being set in
New York City. Such was the paranoia not just in Britain
but also in France that Eric von Stroheim, an Austrian
actor, was arrested near Paris for "looking like a spy".
Despite his nationality he offered to fight for the French
against his mother country. In the same week a new film
called *An Englishman's Home* went on release. Starring Mary

SHE FELL FOR A SPY—

Mary Maguire, the star of "An Englishman's Home."

Maguire, who is "swept off her feet" by a handsome young
foreigner (Austrian-American actor Paul Van Henried) who
poses as a super wireless dealer but is really a spy, the film
tapped into the zeitgeist of the anti-Nazi public.

Lord Londonderry went on record to denounce
those who branded him a spy for, amongst other things,
entertaining von Ribbentrop and Goering as well as
writing a book called *Ourselves and Germany*. His Lordship
defended himself by saying he was making "efforts for
peace in Europe and if only the Government had taken
my advice in 1934 this war could have been avoided".
Londonderry, a bit player in the early years of the conflict
(his talents were little regarded by his cousin Winston
Churchill), quietly faded from public life.

At a more mundane level, on 21 September it was
reported that "spies" in the north of the country were
using cars with false number plates. "Police have enlisted
the help of garages to trace them. One car is a black saloon
with a false number plate. A man sometimes dressed as an
army corporal and sometimes in the uniform of the RAF
has been making enquiries at various observation units
in the Mold (Flintshire) district." Like many such stories
this allegation never featured again, but just added to the
public's overall state of mind…ably assisted over the
coming months by the voice of Haw-Haw.

Spy mania even spilled over into the marital courts where a man who was receiving massage therapy at a local hospital from an Austrian refugee reported that his wife had threatened to "inform his employers that he was associating with a foreign spy". His wife, who denied assaulting her husband, was bound over for two years and fined £20. But by October the courts were in full swing dealing with a story that the *Daily Mirror* headlined as "Big Nazi Spy Ring Story".

It was so farcical that it seemed almost impossible to have been made up. It involved a 23-year-old woman named Treasure Muffett (real name Mable Nellie Muffett) who was accused of assisting a Wilfred Ward to extort money from a Mr X by posing as a German (although she had never left the country), and wearing a badge with the initials SHVK, which was supposed to be the ring's identity – it was in fact her convent school badge (the Convent of the Sacred Heart, Harrow on the Hill). Less than a week later Treasure was found dead in a gas-filled flat in Hampstead, along with the girl who shared digs with her.

Within days further details emerged of the "gay life girls who died starving". It turned out the two girls had committed suicide, were starving (they hadn't eaten for three days), had parties, and Treasure maintained the lie of being German even while working as a nurse, for which she had no qualifications. In the flat was a letter returning £1 that one of the policemen investigating the "spy case" had lent Treasure and her friend, out of his own pocket, so they could eat. Soon after their deaths Wilfred Ward was committed for trial for threatening to expose Mr X as a German spy; Ward was later sentenced to three years "penal servitude".

Other bizarre spy stories concerned a prominent

'TREASURE' DIES IN FLAT

TREASURE MUFFET, the girl who should have given evidence in the Birmingham blackmail case today, was last night found dead in a gas-filled room in a flat at Alexandra-road, Hampstead.

Beside her, also dead, was Miss Maire Williams, aged twenty-two, with whom she took the flat a few weeks ago.

Police believe that the women had beendead for several days. The discovery was made by the owner of the apartment house in Alexandra-road, where the women were living.

She saw water dripping from the kitchenette of the flat and went to investigate. Mrs. Muffet should have attended Handsworth Police Court this morning.

She was to give further evidence in a case in which William Ronald Ward, aged twenty-seven, of Heathfield-road, Handsworth, is charged with attempting to obtain £500 from a Mr. X with menaces.

It had been alleged that Ward threatened to expose Mr. X as a Nazi spy unless he was paid £500.

Giving evidence last Thursday, Mrs. Muffet admitted pretending that she was German and speaking broken English when talking to Mr. X.

Lincolnshire businessman nearly being arrested for being a spy because he suffered from asthma. He had got out of his car near a "well-guarded" site to use his asthma relief, which prompted the guards to call the police. Less than a month later, in the week before Christmas, three men entered the village of Stainton-le-Vale, near to where the asthma attack occurred, and began to talk about local ARP arrangements. They wore the uniform of the St John Ambulance Brigade, in itself a suspicious circumstance (according to the *Daily Mirror*'s irony drenched story). "So the locals allowed the strangers to go on talking, very cleverly telling them nothing of importance, while one stole away to the only shop that has a telephone. There he spoke to the Police. And the villagers kept the strangers talking until the constable arrived. The handcuffs should have clicked as the 'spies' growled 'Foiled again! Curse you, British dogs!' It so happened, however, that the constable knew the strangers as fellow ambulancemen. 'Yes, they were St John's men'.

'There's one thing,' said one of the ambulancemen. 'If there were any spies in Lincolnshire they'd get no change out of Stainton-le-Vale.'"

With Christmas just around the corner spy stories abated. Perhaps, like Hitler, who according to the *Daily Mirror* "had left Berlin", presumably to spend the Christmas holiday in the snow-covered mountain area around Munich and at Berchtesgaden, his mountain retreat.

As the winter of 1939/40 was coming to an end and the realization that serious fighting on the western front was not far off, the spy menace once again got into gear; and this time it was much more realistic and sensible. Ports along the East Coast of Britain from Burntisland in Scotland to Grimsby brought in new regulations to prevent seamen from neutral countries wandering around too freely. Officers from Scotland Yard were drafted into Hull and other ports to assist in their control. It wasn't just the east coast. At a west-coast port a soldier sitting by an open window heard two men outside talking German. When he looked out he saw two men in British uniforms chatting in German. They walked off and were later found sitting a little way away, still talking in German. They pleaded that they were British wireless operators and it was only when they were taken back to their barracks that their story was verified. It turned out they were both learning German so they could "translate Dr Goebbels' propaganda lies for their shipmates."

On 1 April 1940 a story appeared in the *Daily Mirror* that was definitely not a joke. It concerned the large numbers of Austrian and German refugees who had fled to Britain in the pre-war years and how the authorities were concerned that "the great exodus had the Gestapo rubbing their hands in glee. It was the easiest method of getting a spy into Britain." Some 6,000 of the 50,000 refugees in Britain were under police restrictions.

By the end of May this led to "police swooping under the new defence regulations yesterday rounding-up 27 Fascists and Captain von Rintelen, chief of the German spies in the United States in the last war. Twenty-one men

A Home Guard soldier models a wireless set used by enemy agents executed in December 1940. The 2 enemy agents, Jose Waldberg, a German and Karl Meier, a Dutch subject, were convicted at the Central Criminal Court on 22 November.

and four women were detained in London. Most of them are connected with the British Union of Fascists. Captain von Rintelen was staying at the Hampden Residential Club, King's Cross where he had lived since 1935. Mrs Muriel Whinfield, who is among those detained yesterday, lives at Shalden Lodge, Alton, and is prospective Fascist candidate for Petersfield. She is the wife of Lieutenant-Colonel E C L Whinfield, retired. Mrs A Brock-Griggs was one of the two chief Blackshirt organisers in 1937."

A woman buying a packet of cigarettes in a tobacconist shop in London in June 1940 leaves a spare cigarette in a collection box, which will be sent on to a hospital for wounded soldiers.

Our New Prime Minister

In the period leading up to the violation of Dutch and Belgian neutrality there was feverish activity on the political front in Britain. The Prime Minister was feeling the heat from several different directions; members of his own party, as well as the opposition, were getting restless. But it was not something that seemed to unduly bother Chamberlain when he met Reith, Minister of Information, on 3 May. He told him he was confident of his own situation, claiming that Churchill's reputation was "inflated" and mostly based on the reaction throughout the country to his frequent appearances on the radio.

Within a matter of days the situation for Chamberlain proved far from comfortable when a debate was called for by the Labour Opposition to discuss the Norwegian debacle – it was in effect a debate on the Prime Minister's conduct of the war. In the House of Commons on 7 May Chamberlain spoke first, rambling for almost an hour during which time the best he could do was to praise the courage of the soldiers; some called him "dispassionate". Given the aura of defeat that hung around the whole Norwegian campaign it was difficult for Chamberlain to find anything positive to say, but his performance was so uninspiring that at least one ambassador in the Strangers Gallery fell asleep.

Among the members of his own party who spoke out against Chamberlain was Leo Amery, a man not noted for his oratory but who on this occasion surpassed himself. "You have sat too long for any good you have been doing. Depart, I say let us have done with you. In the name of God go!" The following day both Socialist and Liberal MPs were ranged against Chamberlain and two of his closest advisors, Samuel Hoare and Sir John Simon, Chancellor of the Exchequer. Labour MP Herbert Morrison called for all three to resign.

Chamberlain's confidence was unfounded, or perhaps events moved too quickly behind the scenes for the man who had long seemed detached to be able to keep up. Chamberlain's "friends in the lobby tonight" failed to support him in sufficient numbers, and while he won by 281 votes to 200 his majority should have been well over 200 votes.

The 65-year-old Winston Spencer Churchill just before he became Prime Minister.

Too many Conservatives had voted against their leader, or abstained, for him to survive. It was an awful night, with friends from within the Conservatives often voting against their own party – Churchill voted in support of Chamberlain. At just after 1pm on 8 May Neville Chamberlain left the House against shouts of 'Resign!' – but he had other ideas.

For the next 36 hours Chamberlain showed no signs of releasing his grip on power. His only hope of survival was to form a coalition, something he had always rejected. His negotiations with the Labour Party did not go well, but the alternative of Winston Churchill as PM was not popular with the Socialist leadership, or with the rank and file; Lord Halifax had ruled himself out because he felt he couldn't sit in the Lords and be Prime Minister. In the end it was the Labour leader Clement Atlee who told Chamberlain on 9 May that there was no hope for him to continue – neither the Opposition nor the country as a whole, would support him.

The Germans, with impeccable timing, had not been shown a copy of the script because before anything more could happen in London they invaded Belgium and Holland. Events moved fast during the morning of 10 May following a meeting of the War Cabinet at 8am. Ministers reviewed the plans that had been so long in the formulation; Chamberlain's position was very much a secondary consideration. As the morning wore on two more War Cabinets took place, vainly trying to keep pace with events that were unfolding under the German Blitzkrieg. At the third meeting the question of Chamberlain's position was the only thing left on the agenda. A short discussion ended with Chamberlain telling his colleagues that he intended to seek an audience

with the King that evening. Later, George VI and his Prime Minister discussed who should take over the running of the country. The King favoured Halifax, but Chamberlain told him that Churchill was the only choice. At 8.15pm the decision was announced and Chamberlain broadcast to the nation.

The following morning the German invasion put Churchill's appointment as Prime Minister into second place on the front page. The Labour Party issued a statement saying that their executive had "unanimously decided to take their share of responsibility… under a new Prime Minister who could command the confidence of the nation". Sir Archibald Sinclair, the Liberal leader, offered a similar message of support.

Neville Chamberlain had been in poor health for some time. He died six months after his resignation, on 9 November 1940.

The Home Guard

In the days following Churchill's appointment, attention focused on the situation across the Channel. French generals scornfully dismissed reports that the Germans were massing in the Ardennes sector – only to feel the full might of the German tank corps 24 hours later. The Germans soon crossed the Meuse as well as continuing their advance into Belgium: the Allied forces could find no way of countering the speed and power of their advance. The Germans were getting closer.

On 13 May the Secretary for War, Anthony Eden, was tackled in the House of Commons about plans for the defence of Britain if the Germans were to mount a similar campaign to the one they had waged against Holland and Belgium. The fear of an attack by parachutists was uppermost in people's minds, especially given all the press coverage of Germans disguised as civilians, or Dutch, or Belgian soldiers being dropped behind their lines. The following day Eden made an appeal following the 9 o'clock news for "local defence volunteers":

"I want to speak to you to-night about the form of warfare which the Germans have been employing so extensively against Holland and Belgium, namely, the dropping of troops by parachute behind the main defensive lines. The success of such an attack depends on speed. Consequently, the measures to defeat such an attack must be prompt and rapid. It is upon this basis that our plans have been laid. You will not expect me to tell you, or the enemy, what our plans are, but we are confident that they will be effective. However, in order to leave nothing to chance, and to supplement, from sources as yet untapped, the means of defence already arranged, we are going to ask you to help us in a manner, which I know will be welcome to thousands of you.

We want large numbers of such men in Great Britain who are British subjects between the ages of 17 and 65 to come forward now and offer their service in order to make assurance double sure. When on duty you will form part of the armed forces and your period of service will be for the duration of the war. You will not be paid but you will receive uniform and will be armed ... Your loyal help, added to the arrangements which already exist, will make and keep our country safe." **– Anthony Eden, BBC, 14 May 1940**

The response was rapid and overwhelming. In the *Daily Mirror* the following day it was front-page news. The first actual recruit seems to have been in Newcastle where a man arrived within four minutes of the broadcast ending. A man in Surbiton in Surrey said "I rushed to the police station as soon as the broadcast was finished but found a long queue there." By 10pm Surbiton had 100 volunteers, in Edinburgh there were 70 by midnight. There were also large queues outside Hackney, Walthamstow and Chingford police stations, and harassed police sergeants who were without forms telephoned Scotland Yard for instructions. This was the beginnings of what came to be called the Home Guard – Dad's Army!

In the days following Eden's call more news emerged as to how things were to be organized. Women were not to be enrolled and the Local Volunteer Defence Force, as it was initially known, or "para-shooters" as they soon became nicknamed, were to be given a uniform of khaki twill overalls – lighter than the ordinary battledress – and a forage cap. A War Office official said "The officer will be a section commander, a knowledge of weapon handling and a sense of friendly leadership are essential qualifications. Village halls will probably be the headquarters in country districts; drill halls in the towns." What kind of rifles or guns to be issued had not been decided upon, which was unsurprising given the speed with which the force had been set up. But those who already owned rifles (and had licences to use them), sportsmen and rifle club members for example were to take them into service. The War Office spokesmen went on to say: "All the men – crack shots. Ex-Service men and young novices – will be trained. They will not be allowed to take their arms home when the companies are formed."

Sergeant J Stewart, chief instructor of the Home Guard in London's Bow Street, giving training on the correct use of a weapon.

By early June the Government were calling for ex-servicemen who served in the cyclist battalions in the First World War, who were not already serving, to join the VDF to act as dispatch riders. It was also in early June that the VDF were referred to as Home Defence battalions by Anthony Eden in a Commons speech, and a few days later, on 19 June, they had become the Home Defence Services – which, following the fall of France, was considered of paramount importance.

It was not until the end of July that they finally were called the Home Guards; the renaming followed a question in Parliament about the legal status of the volunteers having the "privileges of soldiers".

This is all so reminiscent of the BBC TV series *Dad's Army*, based on a mythical Home Guard unit at Walmington-on-Sea. The series created something of an "Ealing comedy" image of the men of the Home Guard, but at the same time it has also turned them into folk heroes. Given that they were never called upon to perform the tasks that Eden had suggested, this perhaps is hardly surprising.

Just as in *Dad's Army*, there were frequent bizarre incidents for the part-timers to cope with. In August 1940 a Home Guard unit stopped volunteer firemen from getting to the scene of a fire during an air raid because they couldn't produce their ID cards. In true Captain

Para-shootists aged 17–72 meet in the ancient market hall on 3 July 1940 where it is decided which part of the countryside they will be covering as lookouts.

Mainwaring style, the commander of the Home Guard unit was reported as saying: "I have drawn the attention of the battalion commander to the position. My instructions are very definite and we try to carry them out."

In another incident in mid-August initial reports claimed that "A few Home Guards in the South London area were attacked by machine-gun fire from an enemy dive bomber. The Home Guards retaliated with rifle fire, and, after firing 180 rounds, caused the enemy aircraft to crash. This is the first occasion on which the Home Guard have succeeded in bringing down a German bomber."

According to the officer in charge of the Home Guard unit, "I was in charge of the post at the time. All the men had been issued with their rifles and ammunition. My observer noticed the 'plane coming in our direction. He recognized it at once as a German machine, which had evidently been hit. It was flying at a height of about 400 feet. As soon as we had satisfied ourselves that it was an

It was not all hard work in the Home Guard: these three ATS girls, who were living in a caravan, get the attention of the local Home Guard in November 1940.

enemy 'plane some of the men with rifles took up position and we plugged off about 180 rounds into the machine. I gave the order for rapid fire, and my second in command directed the distance and the height of the firing. We saw the machine stagger and lose height, and then smoke began to issue from it. We saw the German 'plane crash between the road on which our posts were situated and the next village."

There seems little doubt that this aircraft was already in serious trouble and it is unlikely that the Home Guard did anything but boost their ego by shooting at it. This mythologizing of the Home Guard stems from the need

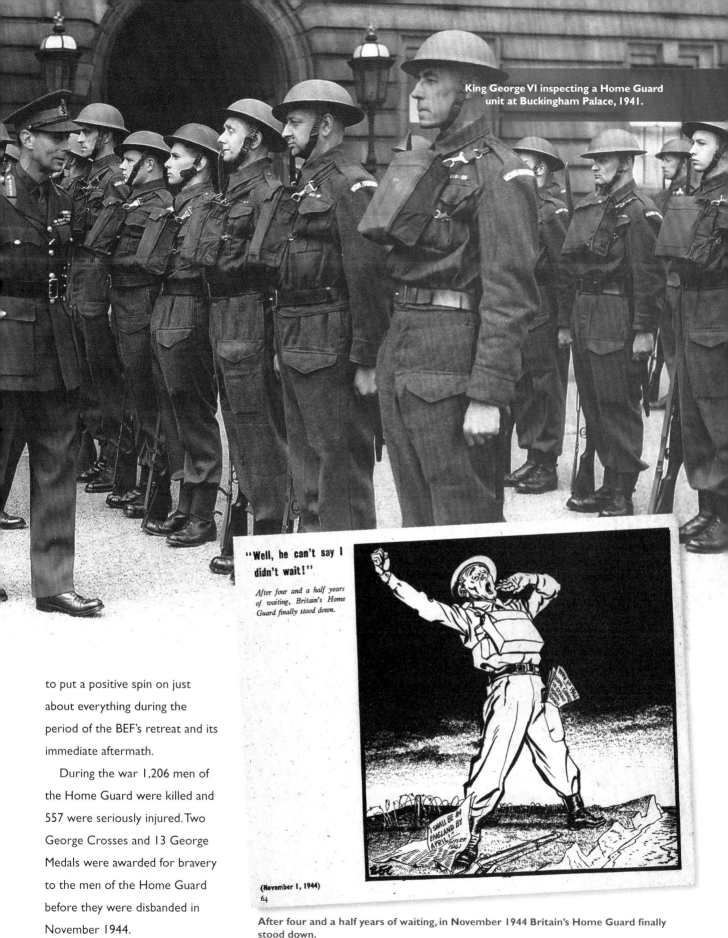

King George VI inspecting a Home Guard unit at Buckingham Palace, 1941.

"Well, he can't say I didn't wait!"

After four and a half years of waiting, Britain's Home Guard finally stood down.

I SHALL BE IN ENGLAND BY APRIL HITLER 1941

(November 1, 1944)
64

to put a positive spin on just about everything during the period of the BEF's retreat and its immediate aftermath.

During the war 1,206 men of the Home Guard were killed and 557 were seriously injured. Two George Crosses and 13 George Medals were awarded for bravery to the men of the Home Guard before they were disbanded in November 1944.

After four and a half years of waiting, in November 1944 Britain's Home Guard finally stood down.

A Miracle

Just before Anthony Eden broadcast his plans on what was to become the Home Guard an Admiralty announcement asked all owners of self-propelled boats between 30 and 100 feet in length to notify the Government within the next 14 days. This was the first sign of the build-up to the Dunkirk evacuation, a clear indication that things were going badly across the Channel.

MOTOR-BOATS WANTED

Anyone who owns a motor pleasure boat between 30 and 100ft. long, which has not already been offered to the Government, must send in details of it to the Admiralty at once.

On 19 May Winston Churchill made his first Prime Ministerial broadcast, the first of nine during the remainder of this crucial year in the defence of Britain.

"I speak to you for the first time as Prime Minister in a solemn hour for the life of our country, of our empire, of our allies, and, above all, of the cause of Freedom."

Churchill finished his speech:

"Arm yourselves, and be ye men of valor, and be in readiness for the conflict; for it is better for us to perish in battle than to look upon the outrage of our nation and our altar. As the Will of God is in Heaven, even so let it be." **– Winston Churchill, BBC, 19 May 1940**

Six days earlier Churchill had given a speech in the House of Commons that showed what he was made of, and that he expected the rest of the country to be cast in the same mould. "I say to the House as I said to Ministers who have joined this Government, I have nothing to offer but blood, toil, tears, and sweat." Everyone at every level was preparing for the worst possible scenario. Ministers made speeches throughout the rest of May and despite their efforts to talk positively, or perhaps because of the intensity of their rhetoric, the mood of the country became intensely gloomy. Children were evacuated from along the coastline facing the Continent; almost everyone, almost everywhere, was preparing for invasion.

Talk was rife that Hitler had a firm date in mind as to when he would invade; some even said they knew for certain that he would drop parachutists inland to disrupt Britain's defences; the Home Guard were sure to be tested. Others talked of how the Luftwaffe would overrun Britain's pitifully small number of modern fighter aircraft. The power of the German Army and Air Force was awesome. Churchill again spoke to the House of Commons saying that the British and French forces would fight on. German Radio announced that British troops were "laying down their arms and fleeing towards the coast". Shortly after the Prime Minister spoke to the House, Lord Haw-Haw's broadcast from Hamburg poured scorn on the Allies. Much of his speech attempted to be divisive, criticizing "those that conducted war from luxury hotels" while contrasting them to those who actually did the fighting.

"The number of British and French prisoners that have been taken is beyond computation." **– Lord Haw-Haw, German radio, 28 May 1940**

Along with the fear of invasion, many families had loved ones fighting in France, which only added to the sense of despondency. Such was the hunger for news that many jumped on any morsel of information that often became even more outrageous in the retelling. The situation in France, and especially in the area around Dunkirk, needed no exaggeration or manipulation, however it was desperate. A German Army that numbered around 750,000 men encircled what remained of the BEF in France. Stuart

Hibberd, one of the BBC's best-known announcers, was returning on the train from London. He noted in his diary: "In my carriage when travelling to Bristol were a number of race-goers, who got out at Bath; they were returning to London again by the 5.40. Nobody seemed in the least perturbed about the serious plight of our army before Dunkirk." Such disregards seems to us surreal, but then again how often when one is not directly involved in something is it easier to blank it, to park it in a part of the brain that allows what counts for normal life, to carry on?

Without television or any of the sort of on-the-spot reporting we are accustomed to today the radio and the newspapers provided the only current reports. However, the more people read or heard, the greater was the fear of invasion. Yet what shone through so much of the reporting at this time was a sense of hope. At the time some would have said it was a triumph of optimism over reality, but hindsight has proven the optimists right. It is impossible to say how much the positive media reporting played a role, even when it was poking fun at the Nazi leaders, in preparing the mindset of Britain for the fight.

As plans were discussed about how to bring the beleaguered troops of the BEF back to Britain on 26 May, it was hoped that the audacious strategy might allow for a few tens of thousands to be saved,

maybe 50,000 at most. When the operation ended on 4 June, over 300,000 men, two-thirds of them British, were saved. Around 34,000 Allied soldiers and airmen were taken prisoner and a similar number killed, along with nine destroyers sunk and over 200 smaller ships lost, many of which were among the boats that had answered the Government's call a few weeks earlier.

Churchill said what had happened at Dunkirk was "a miracle of deliverance". Perhaps the first of several "miracles" that saved Britain.

"It sent shivers (not of fear) down my spine." – Poet and novelist Vita Sackville-West in a letter on Churchill's speech to her husband Harold Nicholson, MP.

The Soldier's Sweetheart

Today it might seem improbable, but many soldiers and airmen from the Commonwealth were eager to enlist to fight against Germany. Similarly, the Australian Government was quick to declare war on Germany and soon imposed conscription on its male population. Australian solders arrived in Britain in early 1940 and were visited by the King at their base in the south of England. Additionally, many Australians became pilots in the RAF and over 100 served with Fighter Command during the Battle of Britain. Their social centre in the Strand Theatre brought many of the soldiers into contact with the local population, and particularly women.

The old cliché about a man in uniform very definitely worked on some young women and gave rise to some interesting letters to the *Daily Mirror*, drawing this fascinating response from the paper's very own psychologist:

"You remember the girl who wrote to the Daily Mirror last week asking whether she was a cheap little cheat because she'd 'got off' with an Australian soldier who gave her the glad eye and asked her to take pity on him? The Aussie said that English

Australian troops on their first London leave heading towards their new social centre at the Strand Theatre in Aldwych, London.

girls were hard to get to know. When one of these stalwarts from down under gave a girl the glad eye, she usually turns on the refrigerator.

I don't know whether this is true of most English girls, but I do know that there are a number of girls who are afraid to meet strange men. Consequently we have in our midst a number of really attractive and altogether nice girls who suffer more hell from loneliness than many soldiers do from dive-bombers.

After a while these girls become obsessed with the idea that all real men are monsters, and force themselves into a state of isolation in which they refuse to budge until Mr Right comes along – if he ever does!

These girls suffer acutely with one or more of the many complexes which create suppressions.

It is not that this particular type of girl does not really want to meet a strange man. In fact, many of them inwardly yearn 'to know certain types' to whom they are naturally attracted.

But the trouble is that they are tied up mentally. Thus instead of deciding to do what they really want to do, they adopt the opposite course, giving the would-be wooer such a frigid stare that he shivers, and while the girls are doing so, they actually feel as cold as they look. Why, you ask, do girls deny themselves the great opportunity for romance?

There are so many potential causes that it is impossible to enumerate them here. One of the main causes, however, is a sense of guilt. People who suffer with a sense of guilt are slaves to convention. As it is not considered to be 'ladylike' or proper to be picked up in the street, they create a case against being picked up if a gay Lothario attempts it, and end with either having the unfortunate man arrested or 'freezing him out'.

But later, when the sense of guilt has passed, and, they think of his sparkling brown eyes, his curly hair and his flashing white teeth, they say to themselves: Perhaps I was a fool. He seemed quite nice.

As a matter of fact most of our behaviour to the world outside of ourselves more often than not exemplifies just the opposite to what we really feel.

That is why a person who is apparently unkind is really very kind, but he persists in being unkind because he believes that the world in general expects him to be that way.

Therefore the girl who turns down a gay Lothario when she really wants him, is pandering to what she feels the world expects of her. . . That is why so many girls find themselves on the shelf."

And this was before the Americans arrived. . .

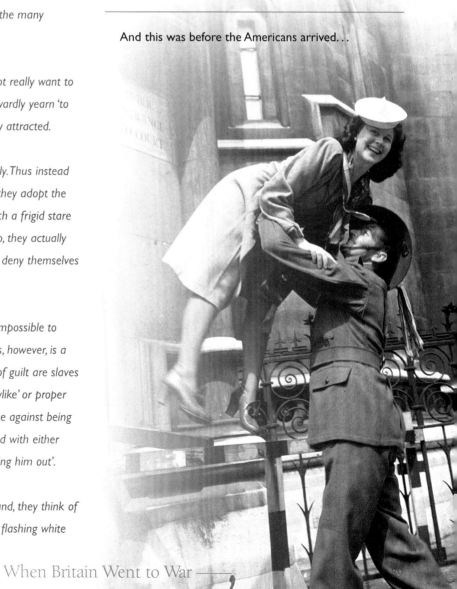

S Class submarines of the Royal Navy tied up alongside a depot ship in September 1940. They are left to right: HMS Sealion, HMS Snapper and Sunfish.

The Battle of Britain

On 14 June the Germans entered Paris, and within 48 hours the new French Premier, Marshall Pétain, sued for peace. Things looked bleak for Britain. Other than the Channel what was stopping the Germans from an immediate invasion? Those who had been saying that Hitler had the date of the invasion already planned may just know what they were talking about. On 17 June Churchill broadcast to the nation saying that Britain expected France would rise again. He finished his statement with words of hope, words that are the very essence of Churchillian greatness – simple, effective and totally understandable by everyone. Politicians today try to emulate him, to copy his style; but he had the power of alchemy – they do not.

"We are sure that in the end all will come right."

The following afternoon Churchill spoke to Parliament once again, cajoling, demanding and seeming once more to conjure up mystical powers to ensure that no one failed to comprehend what was at stake.

"What General Weygand called the Battle of France is over. I expect that the Battle of Britain is about to begin. Upon this battle depends the survival of Christian civilization. Upon it depends our own British life, and the long continuity of our institutions and our empire... Let us therefore brace ourselves to our duties, and so bear ourselves that, if the British Empire and its Commonwealth last for a thousand years, men will still say 'This was their finest hour'." **– Winton Churchill, BBC, 18 June 1940**

In response to Churchill's speech the *Daily Mirror* had this to say on its front page:

"You need not worry about the men and women of Britain, Mr Churchill. The common people of the land have the courage. Give them arms and give them leadership and they will not fail as they have been failed. But Above All Give Them — Leadership."

The Battle of Britain began on 10 July 1940, on that everyone agrees. However, ever since there has been debate amongst historians as to how long it lasted and how many phases of battle there were. The first stage was one during which the Luftwaffe tested Britain's defensive capabilities. They attacked ships in the Channel, mounted small raids on the north of England and sent over reconnaissance aircraft to probe and test the preparedness of the RAF fighters. For the Germans, every RAF fighter lost was one less with which Britain could defend herself. Besides examining Britain's defensive capabilities the attacks on Merchant Navy convoys in the Channel helped to rob Britain of valuable food and materials.

Under threat of invasion, one of the many roads in the south of England closed off and protected by barricades at which cars were stopped and all identification cards shown.

Battle of Britain Day One

The first day of the battle was very cloudy, with intermittent showers. Shortly before 2pm a large German formation showed up on the radar; it was just west of Calais heading towards the Kent coast. There were almost 80 aircraft in all, including 24 Dornier 17s and the rest a fighter escort of around 30 Me.110s and a similar number of Me.109s. The British response was first to scramble Hurricanes from Manston and Biggin Hill in Kent as well as from London's old "London airport" at Croydon in Surrey, along with Spitfires of 74 Squadron from Hornchurch, Essex; later on around half a dozen Spitfires were also sent up from Kenley in Surrey.

While the Hurricanes of 111 Squadron from Croydon attacked the Dorniers, who themselves were busy attacking the convoy, the remaining fighters engaged the escorting fighters. With so many aircraft the sky quickly became a mass of vapour trails, and soon aircraft were going down. Later that day a force of around 70 bombers attacked both Swansea and Falmouth. During the night bombs were dropped in a number of locations in the south, and on the Isle of Mull in Scotland. RAF losses for the day amounted to eight aircraft, with two pilots killed. The Luftwaffe lost 20, which included badly damaged aircraft, and lost 23 aircrew either killed or missing as well as 10 more wounded; one of the ships in the convoy was sunk.

"I was just turning round when I saw an Me. 109 come hurtling at me. He came from above and in front of me, so I made a quick turn and dived after him. I was then at about 5,000 feet and when I began to chase him down to the sea he was a good 800 yards in front. He was going very fast, and I had to do 400 miles an hour to catch him up, or rather to get him nicely within range. Then, before I could fire, he flattened out no more than 50 feet above the sea level, and went streaking for home. I followed him, and we still were doing a good 400 miles an hour when I pressed the gun button. First one short burst of less than one second's duration, then another, and then another, and finally a fifth short burst, all aimed very deliberately. Suddenly the Messerschmitt port wing dropped down. The starboard wing went up, and then in a flash his nose went down and he was gone. He simply vanished into the sea."

– An RAF Flying Officer talking about the first day of the Battle of Britain on the BBC

The importance of these first-hand accounts, which began to appear regularly on the radio, cannot be underestimated in bolstering the spirits of the civilian population.

Scramble!

Air Raid Alphabet

On the first day of the battle the *Daily Mirror* included an "Air Raid Alphabet" in the paper to keep the civilian population up to speed on what to do with the increasing number of air raids. While it is clear that people were expecting the worst there is a strong element of keeping the spirits up and little indication of how difficult it was to become for the civilian population over the coming months. For some bizarre reason the *Mirror* left out J — perhaps it stood for Jerry!

A stands for Air-ring. A perfect blessing when you have to sit for hours in a shelter on one chair. You buy this at the chemist's and blow it up as and when you want. And for Amusements: cards, dominoes, chess — anything quiet to pass the time.

B stands for your Blanket. Always take one along with you, especially at night. And for that Bucket of Sand, which should be kept close at hand.

C stands for Chewing-gum and Chocolate (plain). For a Cushion, too, if you've no air-ring.

D stands for the Doctor you certainly don't want. So, keep under cover, keep dry and keep warm. Also for Damp Feet. Avoid them like the plague!

E stands for your Ears. Plug them well with lightly with vaselined cottonwool when bombs are about. It's also for Entrance (to the shelter). Remember to screen it in.

F stands for First Aid Case of bandages, lint, disinfectant (made-up), pins, smelling salts, tannic acid jelly, bicarbonate of soda lotion, labels and pencil. For the forty winks too, to make up for lost sleep the next day.

G stands for Gas mask, which you always carry with you. And for (household) Gas. Don't forget to turn yours off at the main before taking refuge.

H stands for Hot Drinks. Not tea, we're economising; not coffee — it keeps you awake (so does tea!). Cocoa, malted milk or gruel are ideal. Prepare yours ready in a vacuum flask over night. Also for Hot Water Bottle — your best friend in a shelter.

I is for Identity Card and Idle talk. Have the one with you and dismiss the other. For Injury, too, but treat it at once and keep the patient very warm.

K stands for Knitting, which will soothe your nerves (and if it's for the troops, will be patriotic as well) K is also for clean 'Kerchiefs. Stuff three or four into your coat pocket; you may need them — large ones.

L stands for Lights-out. No more need be said. And, for

Women spotters with an identification chart. Books like the one above were also produced in large numbers in order to make everyone aware of who was friend and who was foe.

night). A warm coat and a pullover (in the day).

P stands for Panic. Remember, you're BRITISH, and we British keep calm. P, too, is for Pluck – an inborn quality that you and all of us, deep down, possess.

Q stands for Quake, Queasy and Quarrel. Three very strong don'ts!

R stands for Return to Bed. A hot drink, a hot bottle, a calm mind and then sleep – don't worry. A few broken nights won't do any harm, for lost sleep is soon made up. R stands for Rest also. A little extra next day or go to bed early should be your rule.

S stands for Sirens. Take cover when they begin, and stay put till the "All clear". S stands for Sedative, too. Should you feel you need one; a hot drink is safest and best on your own unless your doctor has already prescribed.

T stands for Thirst. Something warm and sweetened with glucose is fine. Avoid alcohol, which makes you chilly afterwards.

T stands for Table also. A folding one if possible, as it's there when it's wanted, and gone when it's not.

U stands for Unerring (what you should be) and Unhappy (what you shouldn't).

V for Vacuum Flask.

W for your Warm Wrap (blanket, quilt or coat).

V, Y and **Z** stand for the etceteras.

your Latchkey, Don't leave that behind.

M stands for Money. You may well want a few pence. M is also for the Mattress, which should be in every private shelter, when it's possible.

N stands for Nerves. Remember, they're catching, so don't get an attack. And for your Novel, which is O.K. In the daytime, but don't read at night. You want to keep drowsy, not too alert and wide-awake.

O stands for Outfit. Warm vest, stockings, stout shoes, siren suit, muffler, cosy overcoat and a blanket (at

Identifying aircraft – friend or foe – became something of an obsession.

The Fighter Pilot as Hero

The threat of invasion created the need for heroes, and in the first week of the Battle of Britain the country got its first, a man who would become a legend, immortalized on film in 1956 in *Reach For The Sky*. Douglas Bader had lost his legs in a flying accident in 1931. In June 1940 Bader took command of 242 Squadron, a Canadian unit that had suffered heavy losses in the Battle of France and whose morale was at a low ebb. Bader quickly turned the squadron into an effective fighting unit with some simple rules:

- If you have the height, you control the battle.
- If you come out of the sun, the enemy cannot see you.
- If you hold your fire until you are close, you seldom miss.

242 Squadron became a part of 12 Group based at Duxford, and with the support of Air Vice Marshall Trafford Leigh-Mallory, Bader's "Big Wing" was adopted by Fighter Command. This tactic was to get as many planes in the air as possible in advance of the Luftwaffe getting to Britain, giving Fighter Command height and numbers to overpower the enemy. In early 1941 Bader was promoted to Wing Commander and moved to Tangmere.

He became Britain's first fighter pilot hero, and when he was shot down in August 1941 and taken to a German POW camp his loss was felt across the nation.

BBC Broadcasts – Channel Air Fight

Also on the front page of the *Daily Mirror* was a report about one of the first ever BBC broadcasts covering real war "live". Charles Gardner was heard on the BBC's 9 o'clock news on 14 July.

"A running commentary on the air battle over the Straits of Dover in which seven enemy planes were shot down was broadcast by the BBC last night. An observer standing on a cliff top saw German dive bombers attacking a convoy. Suddenly Spitfires appeared. His voice shaking with excitement, the announcer described the progress of the fight in the style of a Derby or Cup final commentary.

Once the microphone seemed to shake and a crash was heard. 'That,' said the announcer, 'was a bomb.' He might have been saying 'That was a goal.' At one moment the fight was right overhead, 'They've got one,' he shouted. 'The pilot's baled out. The plane's roaring down. It's crashed.'"

As the first "ring-side" commentary at a dogfight, Charles Gardner's excitable voice met with mixed reactions. Several letters to *The Times* were less than complimentary: "As a pilot in the last War, will you allow me to record my protest against the

eye-witness account of the air fight over the Straits of Dover given by the BBC… Some of the details were bad enough; but far more revolting was the spirit in which these details were given to the public. Where men's lives are concerned, must we be treated to a running commentary on a level with an account of the Grand National or a cup-tie final?" wrote R H Hawkins from Dalston Vicarage, Carlisle. Another writer from London agreed with Mr Hawkins, going on to say: "The BBC's standard of taste, feeling, understanding, and imagination is surely revolting to all decent citizens."

A letter-writer to the *Mirror* from Ashington in Northumberland calling himself "Anti-Jitters" said: "It was positively refreshing to contrast the quiet dignified Press reports of Sunday's air raid on the southeast coast with the hysterical commentary which the BBC broadcast. Haven't the relatives of our brave airmen enough anxiety without having to listen to this nerve-racking stuff?"

In response, the editor of the letters page suggested: "If you haven't got the nerve to listen to Messerschmitt

being chased all over the sky – and into the sea – we presume you'd fall into a drivelling mass on the floor if a parachutist landed within 50 miles."

The only pilot to win the Victoria Cross during the Battle of Britain was 23-year-old Flight-Lieutenant James B Nicolson, of 249 Squadron. On 16 August, and although twice wounded, he refused to jump from his blazing Hurricane until he had destroyed his enemy. He is seen here playing shove halfpenny while recovering in hospital.

War of Words

Throughout July the increased threat of invasion bought forth letters to the paper on all sorts of subjects, including suggestions on how to repel the German invaders.

Mr E E GOLDSMITH, of Mount Ephraim, Tunbridge Wells, writes:

*"Cannot we be given some idea of the differences between German and British parachutes and what documentary evidence we can ask for to establish the identity of a suspected parachutist who might have landed in **a** British uniform?"*

C T W. of Ashford, Kent, writes:

"Should we not rid ourselves of the fear of invasion by building a Maginot Line all round Britain? Behind it we could have two or three lines of concrete barricades for the troops to fall back on."

Miss B HEATH, of Low Hill, Wolverhampton, writes:

"Advice, please. I have a perfectly wonderful suit of armour, helmet, gauntlets, and dozens of gadgets. Should I give it up for scrap or sleep in it at night? I could leave the helmet off till the last minute."

Mr H O'NEILL, of Church Road, Willsdon, writes:

"When the war started and the danger of invasion was first seen, a suggestion was put forward that explosives could be embodied in darts. I think that this would make a very effective weapon, but it seems to have been forgotten after all this time."

"FIG" of Ware, Herts, writes:

"A brain wave! Why not convert every field into a concentration camp? Then when the parachutists arrive, we've got 'em where we want 'em!"

"JACK" of Somewhere-in-England writes:

"Lord Beaverbrook was due to visit a certain aircraft factory at 12.15. At that time the workers stopped production to listen to him over the loudspeakers. He eventually arrived at 12.55. The workers had been waiting all that time, then his Lordship spoke for twelve minutes and Sir Hugh Dowding spoke for another ten minutes. Is this the win-the-war attitude?"

"We have just been drafted to a new unit and the Colonel has asked us all to give three pence each to buy a wedding present for his daughter. Three pence each! When his daily cigar money is more than we get a week."

"THE GOONS" of Rochester, Kent

Could this be Gunner Spike Milligan? It was written to the *Mirror* **on 25 July 1940 when he was stationed in Kent.**

"We save paper, cardboard, metal, and so on, but why do we waste thousands of yards of cloth by letting boys of under sixteen wear long trousers instead of shorts? Let the boys of Eton be the first to reform."

"The air raid warnings here often seem to come at meal times. Do you think the Nazi airmen are sent at these times so that the meals of those who don't return will be saved?"

"I suggest that instead of leaflets, hundreds and hundreds of brilliant red, white and blue flags are dropped over France! Think how disconcerting it would be to the Germans to find Union Jacks all over the place!"

The scene at an Edinburgh Scrap Iron Depot where mothers took their prams for use in the war effort. The metal from these prams could be recycled into a Spitfire.

Long Hot Summer

Early in August the threat of increasing air attacks by the Luftwaffe was front-page news in the *Daily Mirror*. On Tuesday 6 August the headline ran "Why Hitler Has Waited So Long". The gist of the article was that Germany was training more and more crews and soon instead of 50 to 100 bombers the numbers of aircraft launched against Britain would run into the hundreds, and whereas nighttime attacks had been relatively ineffective these massed raids would prove far more successful. This all followed Hitler's Directive No.17 issued on 1 August:

"The Luftwaffe will use all the forces at its disposal to destroy the British Air Force as quickly as possible. 5 August is the first day on which this intensified air war may begin, but the exact date is to be left to the Luftwaffe and will depend on how soon its preparations are complete, and on the weather situation."

It was on 8 August when a real shift in emphasis took place and fighter bases in the south of England came under attack, along with the radar stations that were a vital cog in directing the Spitfires and Hurricanes to be in the right place, somewhere close to the right time. If the German's "Operation Sealion", the invasion of Britain, was to become reality it was imperative that RAF Fighter Command should cease to exist. German intelligence reports that filtered back to Berlin stated that the Luftwaffe had drastically reduced the RAF's strength through their actions, and so the date for "Sealion" was set for 15 August.

Throughout this period RAF losses were heavy. Increasingly, pilots who had only just joined a squadron would be thrust straight into battle. Given that sometimes they had as little as 20 minutes' training in dog fights, these RAF pilots were more than holding their own. In the middle of the second phase of the battle, when the full might of the German offensive was concentrated on the airfields of southern England, there took place what has become known amongst historians as "The Hardest Day" – 18 August 1940.

The headlines tell of the increasing severity of Luftwaffe raids, even if they are not always accurate.

The German plan was simple, audacious and potentially catastrophic for the RAF as the Luftwaffe set out to destroy the fighter bases at Kenley and Biggin Hill. The headline of 140 to 16 in favour of the RAF is very misleading... in fact wholly inaccurate! From all available research it would seem that the Luftwaffe lost 96 aircraft damaged or destroyed, but the RAF losses were around 50 aircraft damaged or destroyed. There were also 10 British pilots killed and 16 wounded. By this point in the conflict the RAF was destroying two German aircraft at the cost of one of their own fighters. Given that British aircraft were being produced more quickly than German this was on the face of it good news. The only potential problem was the fact that the Luftwaffe started the battle with more than twice the number of aircraft than those at the disposal of Fighter Command.

Two days after "The Hardest Day" Winston Churchill rose from his seat in the Commons to talk to the House on the progress of the war. He spoke of how everyone should be grateful to the airmen who were facing such overwhelming odds yet were "turning the tide of war". The Prime Minister concluded with words that have become synonymous with the battle:

"Never in the field of human conflict was so much owed by so many to so few."

Hitler's failure to launch "Operation Sealion" inspired one of the best cartoons from this period of the war.

The Last of the Few

Hawker Hurricane.

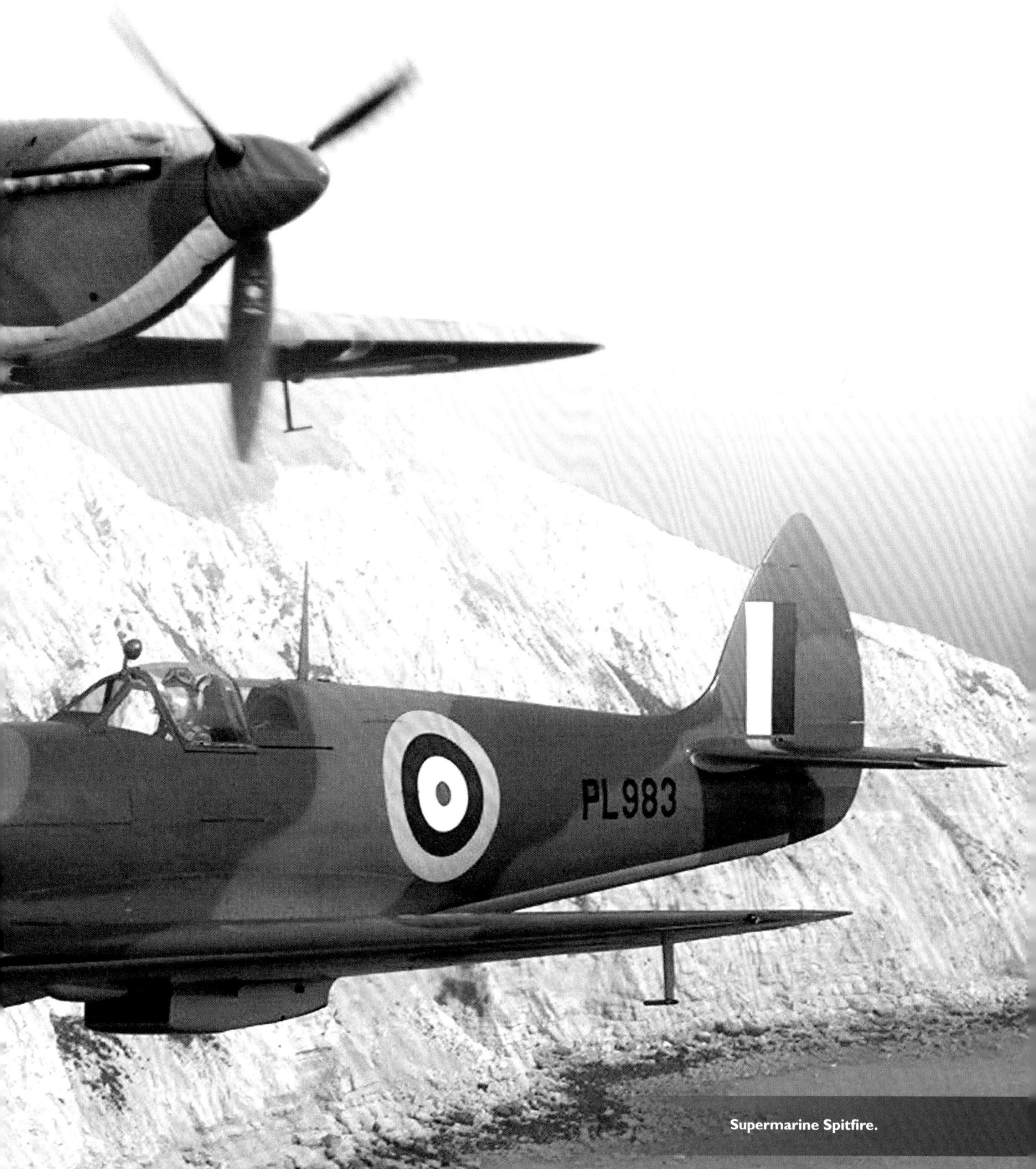

Supermarine Spitfire.

People using Chiselehurst Caves in Kent as a shelter made their own entertainment.

For City and for Country

The Luftwaffe's first attack on London was on 24 August, when St Giles' church, Cripplegate, was damaged. German High Command believed it would break the resolve of the British people if large numbers of civilians were killed. Goering took personal charge of the bombing campaign, justifying it by saying it was in retaliation for British attacks on Berlin. Back home, German secret military communiqués, decrypted by the Enigma machine at Bletchley Park, had given the British Government cause for great alarm: messages indicated that the possibility of an invasion was highly likely – indeed 'imminent'.

The following night's raids again hit London, but far from breaking the resolve of the British people life seemed to go on remarkably ordinarily. At one London theatre Ivor Novello entertained the audience to *Keep the Home Fires Burning* after a performance of his musical *I Lived With You*. At the Duke of York's theatre the manager offered patrons their money back during a performance of *High Temperature* after the air raid warning sounded. Nobody left and the show went on until the end. At others the audience ended up dancing on stage with members of the cast.

By 7 September raids on cities began to reach a new peak. The day had started quietly with no German raiders on the radar. However, by shortly after 3pm the screens lit up. When the Observer Corps made their first sighting of the enemy they quickly realized it was a massive raid; initial reports stated "100 raiders at 20,000ft"; they quickly doubled then trebled this number. In fact these estimates kept on growing and ultimately the raid amounted to around 1,100 aircraft, of which 300 were bombers – the rest made up of their fighter escorts. The damage on London was enormous. The East End of London was set

London was not the only city to take heavy punishment: Swansea suffered three nights of raids in August.

ablaze and the Woolwich Arsenal was just one important factory that was destroyed. Later that night a similar number of Heinkel 111 bombers attacked the still burning city. Almost 500 people were killed and over 1,300 were seriously injured; the Luftwaffe had dropped over 300 tonnes of bombs, to devastating effect. In all, the RAF scrambled 23 squadrons. Losses on both sides were also very large, the final tally standing at over 40 RAF aircraft destroyed or damaged with the loss of 18 pilots. The German losses were 62 aircraft, with 68 aircrew killed.

The need to tell people how well the RAF and the AA guns were doing was vital.

Despite this being so early in the bombing raids, life went on. The old wartime slogan of "Keep calm and carry on" was exactly what people had to do: they needed to "batten down the hatches" and try to live their lives in some semblance of normality. If they hadn't the consequences would have been too terrible to imagine. Fear and panic could have reduced Britain to a state of anarchy. On 9 September, the day after the "Second Night of the Battle of London" as the Mirror's front page reported, there were some quite remarkable illustrations of the fortitude of Londoners.

Elsewhere in the *Daily Mirror* commuters were encouraged to "get to their stations early". British Railways were to do their "utmost to carry all passengers" after workers repaired some damage to the lines. The railways told passengers that there would be "the widest possible flexibility in the use of season or ordinary tickets by any alternative service".

Under the headline "Boobs to Lead Women" there was a forthright attack on putting men in charge of women:

"Women's war services do not seem to want people who have any knowledge of leadership, but choose the 'boobs' every time. Miss Barclay, of Aberdeen, said this at a meeting at St Andrews, Scotland, of the governors of the National Federation of Business and Professional Women's Clubs. A resolution which was passed stated that having regard to 'deplorable conditions of promotion' in women's war services, the Federation wished to emphasise the importance of proper cadet training being enforced for those women with qualities of leaders'. It called on the Government to put this into practice immediately. Mrs Muir (Dundee) said that one of the things women would have to fight, if not during the war, certainly after it, was the movement to put them back into the home. They could not agree with the proposal to put men officers in charge of women in auxiliary services, she said. Women would make as good officers as men, but the trouble was that the picking of women officers in the beginning was done by men. There should not be men medical officers for the women's services, she said."

Women had already been put to work in one area of the war on the home front that was to introduce many to a life far different from what they had been used to before the war. By the late summer of 1940 nearly 50,000 men had been "lost to the land" through enlistment or switching to better-paid work in towns and cities. The Women's Land Army had first been set up in the First World War but was resurrected in 1939 in anticipation of a shortfall in manpower. By August 1940 all the places in

Women employed by the LNER (London & North Eastern Railway) to recover coal dropped by passing trains.

the Women's Land Army were filled.

While the average farm worker earned 38 shillings a week, which in itself was about half the national average wage, Land Girls were paid 28 shillings a week; of this around half paid for board and lodgings. Nor were there any set holiday entitlements, and while many of the girls lived in hostels, some of which were vacant country houses, and had a good deal of fun, there was no getting away from the fact that it was back-breaking work involving long hours, especially in the summer months.

Eventually the number of Land Girls would reach 100,000, but initially the National Farmers Union (NFU) were not in favour of such a move. An article in the *Mirror* in January 1940 did not spell good news for farmers. According to the chairman of the Wisbech, Cambridgeshire, branch of the NFU: "God help us! They *will* perhaps do their best, but it will be a poor best compared with the men whom we can send out in rough weather, I do not find any fault with lady land workers, but I do say that they are not equipped for every task. And

they cannot stand the weather." Yorkshire and Lincolnshire farmers urged the Government to exempt all farm workers from military service.

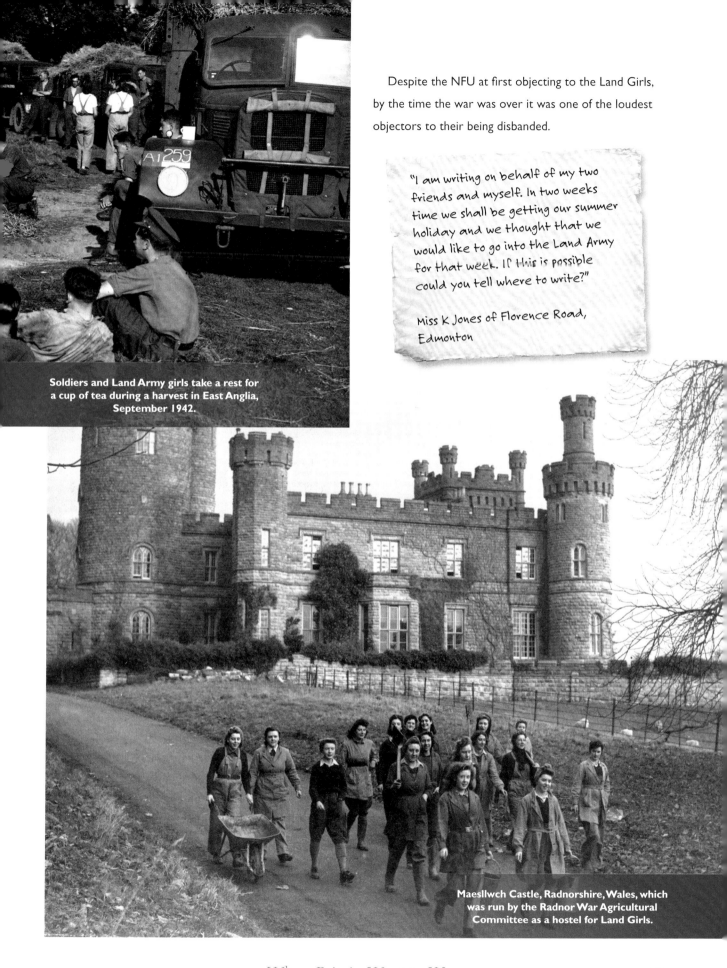

Despite the NFU at first objecting to the Land Girls, by the time the war was over it was one of the loudest objectors to their being disbanded.

"I am writing on behalf of my two friends and myself. In two weeks time we shall be getting our summer holiday and we thought that we would like to go into the Land Army for that week. If this is possible could you tell where to write?"

Miss K Jones of Florence Road, Edmonton

Soldiers and Land Army girls take a rest for a cup of tea during a harvest in East Anglia, September 1942.

Maesllwch Castle, Radnorshire, Wales, which was run by the Radnor War Agricultural Committee as a hostel for Land Girls.

They're Coming!

On 11 September Winston Churchill went on the wireless to broadcast what was one of his most important speeches of the war. Given the severity of the recent raids the need to reinforce the will of the people was paramount; everyone needed to keep fighting, whatever the cost. No one had ever witnessed this type of warfare and there were real doubts as to whether or not Londoners would hold firm – Goering could still be proved right.

Just before his speech Churchill went to inspect the damage in the East End, and while visiting the scene of a direct hit on an air-raid shelter he broke down and cried. Scenes like that were the realities of the bombing campaign, and his main concern was how would people's resolve stand up if the invasion, which was still very

The scene at Buckingham Palace after a daylight raid in September 1940.

much on the cards, were to quickly follow such an aerial bombardment. Churchill used as his theme the Armada, and how it had been repulsed, to demonstrate that when things were at their darkest, victory could spring from the jaws of defeat. The conflicting issues of imminent invasion coupled with the success of the RAF and the fortitude of Britain and Londoners in particular were the interlocking themes of the Prime Minister's broadcast.

He spoke of hundreds of self-propelled barges being readied to carry an invasion force and how "every man and woman will therefore prepare himself to do his duty, whatever it may be". He finished by saying "that we shall rather draw from the heart of suffering itself the means of inspiration and survival, and of a victory won not only for ourselves but for all; a victory won not only for our own time but for the long and better days that are to come".

During the raids that occurred during the night following Churchill's speech Buckingham Palace was hit. Queen Elizabeth said as she visited families bombed out in the East of London, "I'm glad we have been bombed I can now look the people of the East End of London in the eye."

On Sunday 15 September it was a fair day with some patchy cloud, all in all perfect weather for an attack. The Luftwaffe intelligence officers told the German crews that RAF Fighter Command was by now an ineffectual force. The German battle plan called for two major raids on London, with smaller raids on the Southampton and Portland areas later.

According to the RAF Campaign Diary the first attack on London was launched around 11.00 hours as enemy aircraft began to mass in the area between Calais and Boulogne. At 11.30 hours the leading wave of 100 aircraft crossed the English coast between Dover and Dungeness, followed by a second wave of 150 aircraft. The RAF's No 11 Group sent up 16 Squadrons to meet the attack and approximately 100 enemy aircraft succeeded in reaching Central London. The second major attack began at 14.00 hours when approximately 150 enemy aircraft crossed the coast near Dover, followed by another wave of 100 aircraft. These formations spread over south-east and south-west Kent and the Maidstone area; about 70 penetrated Central London. Again No 11 Group sent up 16 Squadrons and No 12 Group 4 Squadrons.

According to the RAF they destroyed around 176 enemy aircraft (the exact numbers vary according to the reports, some giving 179, the BBC News on 16 September stating 185 aircraft) plus 41 probable and 72 damaged. The

Nurses and patients watch the dogfights between the RAF and the Luftwaffe on 6 August 1940.

RAF losses were put at 25 aircraft with 13 pilots killed or missing.

Such was the ferocity of the RAF attacks upon the bomber groups that they succeeded in breaking up the formations, which meant the German aircrafts' bomb loads were spread far and wide across London and the suburbs, causing far less damage than if they had been concentrated. This raid turned out to be a lot less effective from the Nazi perspective than some of the raids earlier in September. Almost as important as defending the capital was the fact that the Spitfire and Hurricane pilots successfully safeguarded Southampton and the Luftwaffe failed to damage the vitally important Woolston factory where Spitfires were made.

In reality the German losses were somewhere between 60 and 80 aircraft. Even if, as was likely, the lower figure was the most probable, this was still the Luftwaffe's worst day since 18 August; generally, the confusion of battle accounted for the exaggerated figures. Different pilots often claimed the same kills and ground gunners were also mistaken in their claims, sometimes thinking they had shot down an aircraft that was already on its way to crashing. RAF losses were around 30 aircraft, with 13

pilots killed. What makes the RAF pilots achievement all the greater is the fact that by this time the average level of combat experience was woefully inadequate. Many of the experienced pilots had been killed, or were recovering from injuries, and while pilots were receiving better training it was no substitute for the real thing. For the German pilots who had been told that the RAF was a spent force the truth was discovered in the hardest way imaginable. Such was the success of the RAF that 15 September has been commemorated ever since as "Battle of Britain Day".

While this day marked the end of any realistic hopes that Hitler may still have had to invade Britain before the autumnal Channel gales set in, it did not bring to an end the daylight raids on London, or the attacks on the fighter bases around London and throughout the south-east. This phase of the battle lasted until the end of September, at which time there was a switch to nighttime bombing raids that achieved little in terms of military value for the Germans. All it did accomplish was to see more and more Luftwaffe aircrew lose their lives. By the end of October the Battle of Britain would be over... but the Blitz was still to reach its climax.

"The Few"

There were 2,353 British and 574 pilots and aircrew from overseas who flew in the Battle of Britain. Some 544, almost one in five, lost their lives during the period of the battle. A further 791 were killed in action or died in the course of their duties before the war's end, making it almost 50 per cent of pilots who fought in the Battle of Britain vwere killed during the Second World War. It was a remarkable achievement, an extraordinary display of courage and heroism, on a scale we are never likely to see again.

"The Battle of Britain ranks in importance with Trafalgar, Salamis, the defeat of the Spanish Armada and other battles of the past in which the invading forces of a seemingly invincible monarch or dictator have been beaten back and which have formed a turning point in history." **– George Orwell, 19 September 1942**

1940-1941
The blitz

The end of the Battle of Britain and the beginning of the Blitz overlapped. For people in Britain the intensity of the German air raids grew over the latter part of 1940 and after a brief winter lull increased again in the early summer of 1941. The strain on Britain's resources from German attacks on convoys in the North Atlantic was tremendous and life for those on the home front became even harder with necessities from food to clothing in increasingly short supply. The war seemed to be being fought on everyone's doorstep.

"Tonight, as on every other night, the rooftop watchers are peering out across the fantastic forest of London's chimney pots. The anti-aircraft gunners stand ready. I have been walking tonight – there is a full moon, and the dirty-grey buildings appear white. The stars, the empty windows, are hidden. It's a beautiful and lonesome city where men and women and children are trying to snatch a few hours sleep underground."

– Ed Murrow, CBS News broadcast to America, 20 September 1940

View of the City of London taken in December 1940 from the roof of St Paul's Cathedral showing the devastation during the Blitz.

1940-1941

7 September	The start of the Blitz on Britain
17 September	Hitler calls off planned invasion of Britain
27 September	Germany, Italy and Japan sign tripartite pact
30 September	Last heavy daylight raid on Britain
16 October	Heavy North Atlantic losses from U-boats over a four-day period
28 October	Italy invades Greece
31 October	British troops land in Crete
14 November	The air raid on Coventry
9 December	Allies begin drive to push Italians back across Libya
16 December	Biggest RAF raid on Germany to date
29 December	Massive air raid on the City of London
12 February	General Rommel arrives in North Africa to take command of Axis forces
2 March	RAF raid on Cologne
7 March	British and Australian troops land in Greece
13 March	Big German raid on Glasgow's Clydebank
17 March	Start of the mobilization of British women for essential "war work"
31 March	After winter lull German raids on Britain intensify
13 April	Japan and Russia sign non-aggression pact
27 April	Germans occupy Athens
1 May	Heavy raids on Liverpool
9 May	Enigma cipher machine and code books captured on a U-boat
10 May	Largest ever raid on London
20 May	German parachutists land on Crete
27 May	*Bismarck* sunk, ending German battleship operations in the Atlantic
1 June	Clothes rationing in Britain
	Allied evacuation of Crete complete
8 June	Largest RAF raid on Germany to date
22 June	Start of Germany's "Operation Barbarossa" to invade Russia
1 September	Siege of Leningrad begins
19 September	Kiev falls to Germans
18 November	British attacks catch Rommel by surprise
26 November	First supplies reach Leningrad since start of siege
6 December	Russian counter-offensive begins near Moscow
7 December	Japan attacks Pearl Harbor
8 December	Britain and America declare war on Japan
13 December	German withdrawal from Russia ordered, countermanded by Hitler the next day
18 December	Japanese forces land on Hong Kong Island
25 December	Hong Kong surrenders

Coffins borne on fire appliances during the funeral of a Plaistow fireman killed in the Blitz.

A Different Kind of War

As the Battle of Britain reached its climax, the RAF was establishing its supremacy, if not winning outright. Postwar analysis of the number of aircraft lost in the Battle of Britain as reported by the British media, and particularly the BBC, which to be fair reported more in "real time", has them overstating British successes by between 50 and 60 per cent, while the German media exaggerated their claims of "enemy kills" by over 200 per cent. While this is understandable, it was also valuable in maintaining the morale of British civilians. The need for morale-bolstering reached a whole new level with the increasing intensity of the Blitz.

As late summer turned to autumn, and then quickly to winter, the German bombing raids continued to inflict casualties on the civilian population. Lord Haw-Haw did his best to talk up the Luftwaffe's success and in so doing boosted the will to resist because of the absurdity of his claims. His prediction of imminent collapse, which of course never came, was at the root of his barmy rhetoric:

"We have learned with horror and disgust that while London was suffering all the nightmares of aerial bombardment a few nights ago, there was a contrast between the situation of the rich and the poor which we hardly know how to describe. There were two Londons that night. Down by the docks and in the poor districts and the suburbs, people lay dead, or dying in agony from their wounds; but, while their counterparts were suffering only a little distance away, the plutocrats and the favoured lords of creation were making the raid an excuse for their drunken orgies and debaucheries in the saloons of Piccadilly and in the Café de Paris. Spending on champagne in one night what they would consider enough for a soldier's wife for a month these monied fools shouted and sang in the streets, crying, as the son of a profiteer baron put it, 'They won't bomb this part of the town! They want the docks! Fill up boys!'"
– Lord Haw-Haw, late August 1940

It wasn't just air raids that affected the civilian population. In mid-September German long-range guns were shelling a convoy from their French-based batteries when some of the shells actually fell on Dover. Eleven people were injured on the first day of this shelling that kept up until 1944 when the advancing Allies captured the guns. In all, well over 2,000 shells landed on Dover and such was the intensity of attack on the Kent coast that it became known as "Hellfire Corner".

The scale of the damage inflicted on London is difficult to imagine for those used to seeing the city today.

Going Underground

The vast majority of Londoners took to the shelters during the nightly air raids. Some went to one of the 79 large public shelters in London Underground stations while others used Anderson shelters, which they erected in their own gardens. Other shelters were built to accommodate people from a nearby street or block of flats. In these people would do what they could to make the shelters a home from home. Some even pinned pictures of film stars on the walls.

While many of the shelters did their job, some were not so well made, nor were many capable of taking a direct hit. Early in September 1940 a report in the *Daily Mirror* tells of a tragedy in stark and harrowing detail:

Aldwych Underground station.

"Scores of families were settling down in a big underground shelter in an East London district on Saturday night, when a bomb hit the only vulnerable spot in the powerfully protected structure. The hit was on a ventilator shaft measuring only about 3ft by 1ft. The rest of the roof was protected by brickwork earth and other defences. But over the ventilator shaft were only corrugated iron sheets.

Mothers were killed before they had a chance to protect their children, babies were swept from perambulators. Three or four roof support pillars were torn down, and about fifty people lay in stunned heaps. About fourteen of them were killed and some forty injured and rushed to hospitals. With bombs still falling, and in the glare of the East End fires, Civil Defence men coolly worked among the debris of the shelter, seeking the wounded, carrying them to safer places, and giving them first aid.

Nine doctors answered an SOS and saved lives by improvising tourniquets. They dressed wounds by the dim glow of carefully held torches. In one family three children were killed. Their parents escaped. A man, when the smoke and noise died down, searched for his wife, found her lying on the ground and turned her over. She was dead. Hours afterwards a woman, her head and arm swathed in bandages, was in the refuge room of the shelter, waiting for news of her two children. She did not know that both were dead.

A.R.P workers said that despite it all there was no panic. 'The women were magnificent' they declared. The Civil Defence men set a superb example. Air Warden Sales said: 'An A.F.S. man ought to get a medal. He flung off his tunic, organised everyone who was unhurt, whether in uniform or not. He seemed to know exactly what to do and what to say, and it was largely owing to his command that all the dead and wounded were cleared out of the shelter in about twenty minutes.'

The fireman was Mr H Beare, an ex- soldier. Yesterday he was searching for a purse which his wife had lost in the wreckage. 'I am not so much bothered about the money, inside it as the ration cards,' he said."

In the month before war breaking out the *Daily Mirror* was regularly a 28-page paper, but by September 1940 it was down to 12 pages (it would drop to eight pages in 1941) — rationing affected everything. Given the shortage of space it often called for brevity, where today verbosity would probably take over. The shortage of space meant that reporting became sharper, and so made the heroism and the tragedy all the more poignant.

Air Raid Precautions

During the Spanish Civil War the German Air Force bombed the town of Guernica, inflicting very heavy casualties that resulted in the Air Ministry predicting dire consequences from Luftwaffe raids on Britain. The Government expected a million people killed and injured in the first month of the war.

The Air Raid Precautions organization, or ARP, was first established in 1924, and by the time war broke out it was extremely well organized. The wardens distributed gas masks, helped build air-raid shelters, assisted the police and the fire service and perhaps most important of all, helped to rescue many thousands of people during the bombing raids.

In the event the Luftwaffe proved less effective than anticipated, with Britain suffering around three casualties for every ton of bombs dropped. No doubt the efforts of the 1.4 million ARP wardens, almost all unpaid part-time volunteers, helped in this regard. They patrolled the streets maintaining the blackout and doused many incendary bombs with sand.

Many wardens went well beyond the call of duty and one of their number, Thomas Alderson from Bridlington, was the first to be awarded the George Cross, the highest civilian award for gallantry.

AIR RAID PRECAUTIONS BADGE

An ARP warden in full protective clothing.

DAILY MIRROR, Wednesday, Oct. 2, 1940.

Daily Mirror

OCT 2

No. 11,467

Registered at the G.P.O. as a Newspaper.

ONE PENNY

Mrs. Jane Bessie Hepburn (left) and Mrs. Dorothy Clarke, Aldeburgh (Suffolk) ambulance workers, who have been awarded the George Medal for rescuing a man who was injured in an explosion.

FIRST WOMEN TO WIN
GM

Three A.R.P. women have won the new George Medal for Valour.

Three—whose honour is the honour of the thousands of women who, by day and night, in the towns and villages, go unfearingly, unflinchingly amid falling bombs, to their self-imposed duty.

Their deeds unsung, often unknown...

Valiant Women of England.

GIRL, 19, AIDS VICTIMS 13 HOURS

FOR thirteen hours a Titian-haired girl of nineteen, a part-time A.R.P. volunteer, helped to save the lives of more than a dozen people injured in a raid.

She had had no practical experience of first aid, but her work won the admiration of experts.

Miss Sonia Straw, of St. Michael's road, Caterham Hill, Surrey, is one of the first three women to be awarded the George Medal.

The two other heroines are Mrs. Dorothy Clarke and Mrs. Jane Bessie Hepburn, ambulance workers of Aldeburgh, Suffolk.

Sonia Straw is a shorthand typist. She works in a solicitor's office.

She had training. She was not trained when she was going out for duty.

After skilfully dressing the wounds of people injured in bombs near her home, she went out into the darkness during a raid—against the advice of fellow A.R.P. workers—to search for a woman missing among wreckage.

She's Qualified Now

She would not give in until the woman had been traced.

Sonia has since qualified in first aid first and is now a fully-fledged warden.

"I do go more than anyone else could have done," she told the Daily Mirror last night.

"I could never stand people lying badly injured. What whatever I could find I bandaged them up.

"I used to think I would be scared at the sight of blood, but all these feelings leave you when you see them in distress.

"Three soldiers brought water and bandages for me, and I soon had all the injured fairly comfortable. They were mainly women and children.

"After I had finished, someone telephoned to say they could not trace their warden, who had been in the bombed part of a flat."

Midnight Search

"With another warden I helped search for her till after midnight. When I found her she was dead under a bed."

Sonia was having a cup of tea when the alarm sounded. Immediately she rushed to her post. An injured woman was a guest in her home and her first patient. The woman was later taken to the wrecked Anderson shelter.

Sonia lives in digs at Caterham, and goes to work at 9.30 every morning and finishes at six.

"Then I go home for supper and sleep in the wardens' rest," she said.

Continued on Back Page, Col. 4

Miss (Air Raid Warden) Sonia V. C. Straw, of Caterham (Surrey), one of the first three women to win the new George Medal. Only nineteen years old, she volunteered, and attended injured women and children while bombs fell round her.

RAIDERS CHECKED

GERMAN night raiders over London again had to run the gauntlet of terrific anti-aircraft fire, and in the early stages of last night's attack big guns turned some of the bombers off their course.

Two which came in from the northwest were turned to swing south before they had reached Central London.

So fierce was the opposition that London had an unexpected All-Clear before midnight—the first since the blitzkrieg started.

The lull had lasted more than an hour.

One of twelve incendiary bombs dropped on a North-West suburb fell near a shelter entrance. A man rushed from the shelter, picked up the bomb which was then alight, and hurled it into the roadway out of danger.

A sixteen-year-old grocer's boy and his brother coolly threw sand and water over other bombs and stamped them out before the fire brigade arrived.

Several German attacks on south-east England and London were resumed during daylight, and four enemy planes were shot down. Three British machines are missing.

The King paid his first visit since the occasion to the Colonial Office during the afternoon.

An air raid warning was in operation when he arrived, but the "All-clear" was sounded during his visit, which lasted nearly an hour.

A Poole (Dorset) fighter shot down three out of a large formation of raiders.

A Messerschmitt 109 came down completely wrecked in a field on the northern outskirts of Brighton. The pilot was dead.

Two other enemy fighters were so damaged by Spitfires in this battle that though they escaped in the clouds their return home is unlikely.

GUARD ON BRIDE

BY A SPECIAL CORRESPONDENT

AFTER she had received two anonymous letters warning her not to go through with her marriage a bride at Trinity, Cornwall, had her home set on fire on the wedding eve.

The bride, Miss Ida Hoskins aged twenty-four, of Collingwood House, was asleep in the house with her mother and two friends but neighbours saw the place ablaze after midnight and warned them.

When the wedding took place next day guests were on guard outside the chapel. Mr. Leonard Lavery, of Kelsey Ford Cornwall, was the bridegroom.

Police investigating the mystery believe jealousy was the fire-raiser's motive. Before she left for the wedding they interviewed the bride in her bridal gown.

Dog Didn't Bark

The bride's mother told the Daily Mirror: "We had been in the house unaware of the wedding until eleven o'clock. Someone must have wanted to set the lights go out, then went across the garden. Neither I nor my daughter can think of anyone who would want to harm her.

"She had been going out with Mr. Lavery for six years and had been engaged to him for three.

"Whoever started the fire must have been known to us, as the dog was outside in the porch and would have barked at a stranger.

"It was a miracle we were not burned to death. We were but taking off our nightdresses and making up our faces, when our neighbours, all in windows that we awoke. They had been playing cards in the house next door and saw the blaze. At first they thought an incendiary bomb had dropped.

"Fortunately, nothing untoward happened during the ceremony. Bride and bridegroom have now gone to St. Austell on their honeymoon."

Air raid wardens set up an information point during an invasion exercise in Kingston, Surrey.

Men wearing gas masks and protective clothing in front of a Newcastle *Evening Chronicle* van.

Air raid warden by roadside sign warning of an air raid in September 1940.

A·R·P WARNING! THE SIRENS HAVE SOUNDED.

Wardens with their gas masks and helmets study race cards in April 1940.

A warden sounds her gas rattle in Kingston-upon-Thames during a gas alarm in April 1941.

An ARP exercise in central London tries to replicate a crashed Nazi bomber in March 1940.

London's Burning

During the bombing of London as many as 136,000 people slept each night in Underground stations, although the number reduced from its peak in October 1940 to around 96,000 in January 1941. The Blitz lasted until May 1941. Around two million homes were destroyed in Britain, 1.2 million of which were in London. Almost 40,000 were killed and over 50,000 people were seriously injured. The majority of those who lost their lives were in London. The devastation to the City of London was terrible with 30 per cent of this historic area totally destroyed. The numbers of people made homeless in the Blitz was enormous, and for some unfortunate people it happened more than once.

A mother tends to her young son while her daughter settles into a bed made from a wooden fruit box in September 1940.

Fires in London's Ave Maria Lane started by high explosive during the Second Fire of London, 29 December 1940.

Firefighters check their breathing apparatus and gas masks before moving into a burning building in November 1940.

Air raid damage in Malden, August 1940.

Firemen in the churchyard of St Paul's Cathedral during the Second Great Fire of London, December 29 1940.

Coventry's Day of Judgment

Besides London, Coventry, Birmingham, Southampton, Bristol and Liverpool were all targeted by heavy Luftwaffe raids before 1940 was over. By the end of May 1941 Cardiff, Glasgow's Clydeside, Plymouth, Portsmouth, Hull, and Belfast all came in for some heavy bombing. But it was the raid on Coventry on Thursday 14 November 1940 that was the most significant outside the capital. In all, 568 people were killed, and another 863 seriously injured, when over 400 bombers dropped 400 tons of bombs on the city centre and industrial areas. Thousands were made homeless and the city's famous cathedral, apart from its spire, was destroyed.

In all, Coventry suffered 41 air raids and according to local records the alert sounded over 370 times; a total of 1,236 people lost their lives in the city during the war. Each British city that was attacked has a similar story to tell, but none, outside London, was as devastating as that one night when central Coventry was all but destroyed.

"It's almost like the day of judgment, as pictured in some of the old books." – **BBC News, 15 November 1940**

The remains of Coventry Cathedral, 15 November 1940.

Rescue workers take names and addresses of those injured in the air raid.

St Mark's Church, Coventry; it was repaired and used as a clinic for Coventry and Warwickshire Hospital.

Coventry railway station.

One of the many badly damaged Coventry streets.

Coventry residents outside their ruined homes.

"The Germans said they 'aimed at the British war plane industry'. They actually hit the cathedral, two churches, a school and public baths." **– Daily Mirror, 15 November 1940**

A model in London at a West End Utility
Fashion show in 1942.

The War on Shabbiness

In September 1940 as the Blitz was getting into full swing there was an announcement on the front page of the *Daily Mirror* that "Undies were to cost more". The price of rayon was increasing so dramatically that stockings and ladies underwear were becoming more expensive. The fact that there was a war on did not dent the enthusiasm of Britain's women for fashion.

According to Kathleen Peachey and Silvaine, writing in the *Mirror* – "Don't let anyone kid you into believing that it's patriotic to look shabby. Too often it's just an excuse for laziness."

The two "fashionistas" were not going to let their readers "slide into that crime".

"She was standing in front of a small mirror hung on the office wall. He sat on the edge of the table discussing orders for the day, asking dull, routine questions. It happened most mornings all the year round. Suddenly he said; 'I admire women like you ... from the bottom of my heart. Here we are after a year of war, spending half our days and nights in shelters, living on a tightrope between life and death; and you still take the trouble to put your hat on properly. You and other women like you put a pattern on life for every man that looks at you in the street, on the bus, right here in the office.'

No... he wasn't falling in love with her, or even paying her a charming compliment. He was saying what nine men out of ten in these grim, grey days want to say when they see a woman who manages to be practical, efficient and decorative. I know women, far too many of them, who are making the war an excuse to be slack about their clothes, their faces and their hair. They slop about in trousers, old sweaters and dirty shoes. You hear them boast how they haven't bought a thing for months, and they don't believe me when I tell them... and I do tell them... that innumerable women are doing without smokes and drinks and bus rides in order to look groomed and charming... not just now and then, but all the time.

Shabbiness, except when it is caused by real poverty, is another word for laziness!"

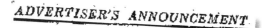

A motorist offers a fashionably dressed young woman a lift while ignoring the old lady, October 1940.

How can you get a GIRLISH FIGURE

WOMEN who have a tendency to put on weight can easily regain a slim, girlish figure with the aid of nightly Bile Beans.

Bile Beans are the safe, healthy way to slimness. Being purely vegetable, they act gently and naturally. Just a couple each night and that surplus fat gradually melts away, leaving slender, graceful lines.

Bile Beans eliminate fat-forming residue daily, and by toning up the system and purifying the blood give you radiant health and a fashionable slim figure. So don't envy others—start taking Bile Beans regularly tonight.

"I soon lost weight when I started with Bile Beans. By taking them regularly each night I have reduced two stones and regained my fitness and energy."—Miss E. M. London, S.W.

"Now I've found the secret of keeping healthily slim, never again will I be without Bile Beans. They have reduced my weight by thirteen pounds. I never felt so well."—Miss E. P. Whitley Bay.

BILE BEANS
Will Make You Healthily Slim

A bride on her wedding day in October 1943.

What we can't Win in War, we will Win in Football!

Despite the impending crisis, when the 1939/40 football season kicked off on 26 August 1939 over 600,000 people watched the games. The following weekend, on 2 September, the games went ahead as planned; but these were the last formal fixtures for the duration of the war. Initially there was a ban placed on the assembly of large crowds, but by 14 September this had been rescinded. However, the number of spectators at any game was limited to just 8,000 (it would later be increased to 15,000).

Clubs were unable to field teams of their regular players as many were called up and transferred overseas with the BEF or to other parts of the country. Bolton Wanderers had 32 of their footballers join the armed forces, the remaining three players went to work in the coalmines. It was a similar story throughout the country.

Players would turn out for clubs depending on where they were based, if they were in the forces, or where they were living and working. The logistics of matches were further restricted because there was a ban on travelling too far to play. The Football Association created regional "leagues" and winners were decided on points averaged rather than total number of points because games were often cancelled at short notice.

A Football League War Cup was organized over the 1939/40 season, the final taking place at Wembley on 8 June with 42,000 people in attendance. West Ham beat Blackburn by one goal to nil. In 1941 Preston and Arsenal drew 1-1 at Wembley in front of 60,000; Dennis Compton, who also played cricket for England, scored the Arsenal goal. The replay at Blackburn was won by Preston by 2

goals to 1. Arsenal's ground at Highbury was closed during the war, so their "home" games were played at White Hart Lane, which must have hurt! Other winners of the wartime cup were Wolves, Blackpool, Aston Villa, while Charlton Athletic shared the cup in 1943/44 and Bolton won the final cup.

These nine members of Bolton Wanderers were all members of the Territorial Army when war broke out. In 1941 they managed to keep together and became part of an artillery battery on the East Coast.

Soldiers watching a game of football on 16 September 1939, after the lifting of the ban.

Auld Enemies

It was not just league matches that were played. England played Scotland in October 1941, with England winning, 2-0 watched by 60,000 at Wembley.

"MATTHEWS WAS THE STAR IN ENGLAND'S VICTORY.

In the English dressing room, after yesterday's international at Wembley, the home country boys were having a word or two to say about Chelsea. England won 2-0. It might have been 3-0 if Chelsea had not lent their nice, modern elliptical goalposts to Wembley.

Donald Welsh sent in a terrific, goal-all-the-way shot and the 60,000 had their mouths wide-open ready to shout the word. The ball struck the under-side of the bar and rebounded a few inches the right side of the goal line – the right side for Scotland that is! Welsh (has anyone ever seen this blond, twinkle-toed marvel from Charlton go through a match without a constant, ear-to-ear smile ?) scored England's first goal, fourteen minutes after the kick-off whistle. After a first-minute shock when Williams missed a chance for Scotland that was sitting up to beg the homesters peppered Dawson with all-angle shots. Matthews and Mannion had shots magnificently saved, and then Welsh finished a grand movement with a typical Welsh snorter.

Second goal came eight minutes before lemon time. Hagan tricked his man before leaving Dawson with a cold in the head from the draught as the ball whistled into the rigging. Cleverest, man afield was Stan Matthews. He was so good that when Bettie did once manage to dispossess tile Stoke City crack, the crack gave the Preston North End full back an appreciative roar and Handclap nil round.

If we dismiss the game as a very nice exhibition, a reminder of things as they used to be, we shall have it in the correct perspective. There was no 'needle' atmosphere to it, but it was certainly well worth watching. Scotland were not outclassed, but they certainly deserved to be beaten. If we are going to sort out individuals, Caskie was their star. His wing runs had everything it takes to keep the fans on their toes, Scotland's trouble was that they muffed so many great chances.

Tommy Walker was offender No. 1. He had one good shot saved by Marks, but just after failed to introduce the ball to the net despite the fact that England's keeper was standing well away from the goal. Anyway, we shall remember this as 'Winston's Wembley'. The Prime Minister obviously enjoyed the game – and I should think the rest of the 60,000."

There were also internationals played in England between players from the occupied countries. The week after England beat Scotland, Belgium beat Holland 5-4 at Wembley.

Freddie Steele and Andy Beattie Steele (2nd left) and James Dawson, the Scottish keeper, during Scotland v England football match on 4 October 1941.

The Scotland team being presented to Prime Minister Winston Churchill.

Manchester United Blitzed

The dangers inherent in holding football matches is clearly seen in these photographs of Old Trafford, Manchester United's ground. In December 1940 Manchester suffered heavy air raids that lasted for two nights, well over 400 tons of bombs were dropped, killing almost 700 people and injuring another 2,364. In March 1941 Old Trafford was hit; the damage would not be repaired for eight years. United returned to Old Trafford in August 1949, having shared City's Maine Road ground in the postwar period.

A view of the Blitzed main stand in 1948, which was later demolished, seen from Popular side.

Holidaymakers sunbathing look pityingly at a passing member of the Home Guard in July 1941.

Mrs Laura Henderson, owner of the
Windmill Theatre, with some of the
Windmill Revue ladies.

Entertainment Tonight

By 1941 the need for entertainment had never been
greater. Having gone from the boredom of the "Phoney
War" to the terror of the Blitz the public wanted and
craved diversions to distract them from the way the war
was going. In cities where the Blitz had been so effective in
affecting all forms of entertainment the wireless was the
main form of entertainment, other than reading, although

in the communal shelters there were often sing-songs and
even dances.

People grabbed any and every opportunity to visit the
cinema, the theatre and dances. The Mermaid Theatre in
the heart of Soho boasted that "we never closed" and
their "tasteful" nude shows attracted not just servicemen
in London on leave but people from all walks of life. Laura
Henderson had originally bought the theatre in the early
1930s and had it remodelled into a small auditorium, but it
proved unprofitable and reverted to showing films.

It became a theatre once more after Vivian van
Damm was hired as manager and in 1932 she came up

STAGE AND EXIT

NO VISITORS ALLOWED IN DRESSING ROOMS AT ANY TIME

with the idea of a Revuedelle, a non-stop programme of vaudeville featuring dancers and showgirls that ran from the early afternoon until 11pm. But this too proved to be unprofitable until van Damm came up with the idea of having nude girls similar to those featured at the Moulin Rouge and Folies Bergères in Paris. The only problem was they were forbidden from moving; and had they done so the censors would have closed the theatre.

Apart from the 12 days when theatres across London were compulsorily closed the Windmill stayed open throughout the war. The cast sheltered in the two underground floors during the worst days of the Blitz.

A Windmill girl kisses her RAF pilot boyfriend backstage in September 1940.

On Air

Today it's hard to imagine a world without television, a world where 24-hour rolling news was unimaginable – but that was Britain during the war. The public's appetite for news went up and down, depending on what stage the war was at. In mid-June 1940, between the evacuation of Dunkirk and the French capitulation, an average of 16.5 million adults listened each day to the 1 o'clock news, although, generally, the 9 o'clock news remained the most listened-to bulletin of the day.

Contemporary research showed that people in the south were far more likely to listen to the news at 9pm than at 6pm – in the north it was the reverse. Overall people living in Scotland listened to more news bulletins than any other part of Britain. However, the newspapers were still a key factor in delivering news to Britain.

Since the early part of the war, when gramophone records and dull information-type programmes had been the order of the day, the BBC had worked hard at creating programmes that were aimed fairly and squarely at entertaining people. Almost 11 million people listened to *Saturday Night Variety* each week. However, with things being so grim on the home front and in the pursuit of the war there was a seemingly insatiable appetite for talks and commentaries. *War Commentary* regularly drew audiences of over 7 million. *American Commentary*, with speakers like Raymond Gram Swing, got close to 6 million listeners on Saturday nights, immediately after the 9pm news, while *In Your Garden* usually attracted around 3 million people most eager to learn how to be more productive in their back gardens or allotments.

One of the biggest successes for the BBC was ITMA; short for "It's That Man Again", "That Man" being the comedian Tommy Handley. With catchphrases like "Can I do yer now, sir?", "I don't mind if I do" and "Ta-Ta for now", which was shortened to TTFN and brought back into common usage by BBC Radio 1 DJ Jimmy Young in

the 1970s, ITMA became an essential part of the BBC's wartime output. It was devised by Handley, a seasoned radio performer, and his scriptwriting partner Ted Kavanagh, and ran for 310 broadcasts – for millions of listeners it was the perfect antidote to the war.

ITMA did not begin during the war but merely carried on, and got better, having first been heard in July 1939. The show's title was lifted directly from a *Daily Express* headline of 2 May 1939 referring to Hitler's pre-war territorial scavenging. The second series began in September 1939, followed by a third in June 1941 – when it briefly became "It's That Sand Again". As well as catchphrases the revolving cast of characters had some wonderfully inventive names. The best was arguably Hattie Jacques who joined the series as "Sophie Tuckshop". ITMA continued in the immediate postwar period and the final series began in September 1948 with the very last show broadcast on 6 January

1949. There was supposed to be one more scheduled ITMA for the following week but tragically Tommy Handley died on 9 January 1949, three days before his fifty-third birthday. The BBC decided the show should not continue – a wise decision, as Handley was ITMA

Comedian Tommy Handley with girls at Jack Hylton's new revue ITMA, premiered in Birmingham in February 1940.

The victims' clothing piled up next to the Palace Dance Hall.

Dance Hall Days

The dangers of the Blitz for people out enjoying themselves were nowhere better illustrated than in March 1941 when the Café de Paris was bombed. The *Mirror* reported the events but for censorship reasons did not reveal the exact location:

"A packed dance hall was wrecked, and a bus and a row of shops and offices were demolished when bombs fell in a London area on Saturday night. Several people in the dance hall were killed, and others were so injured that they died in hospital. At least half the people in the fully occupied bus, and people sheltering in neighbouring doorways were killed. Sixty couples — munitions workers, soldiers on leave and typists — were on the dance floor when four H.E. bombs whistled down. One hit the dance hall, blowing out one end of it. The lights crashed down. Dancers were flung to the floor. Debris cascaded on young couples."

In actual fact 30 people died and around 60 were injured at the Café de Paris on a night when London Civil

Defence records show that 159 people were killed and 338 seriously injured in 238 separate incidents.

This tragedy encouraged one woman to write to the paper condemning what went on. Fortunately this was not a sentiment shared by everyone.

"I HAVE long felt that it is a disgrace to what we call our 'War Effort' that people should fritter their time away dancing night after night. The recent destruction of two dance halls seems like a Divine Judgment on the subject. After all, who can call dancing a 'healthy' recreation? Young men and women herded together, in a stuffy atmosphere, in close proximity to one another, is hardly conducive to the moral wellbeing of the race. I read that the Minister of Home Security is considering closing all dance halls during air raids. So far, so good. I would go further and urge him to shut them after blackout time, anyway.

The spare time of all of us. . . soldiers, sailors, airmen, men and women workers is better spent in healthful sleep or exercise than in flaunting around these haunts."

"WOMAN WAR WORKER" of Huddersfield

The loss of life in the Café de Paris tragedy was small compared to the 73 people, including soldiers and airmen, who were killed at the Palace Dance Hall in Putney in November 1943.

With fewer raids taking place by this time, people were much less concerned about seeking the safety of a shelter. People just kept on dancing even though the air raid warning had sounded.

All that remained of the Palace Dance Hall in Putney High Street.

When the Dance Bands Ruled

Dance bands, and their singers, were the pop music of the 1930s and '40s. Many of the bandleaders were popular from the 1930s and continued providing the soundtrack to the war, both on radio, gramophone record and live at dance halls up and down the country. In May 1941 a story appeared in the *Melody Maker* aimed at winning the hearts and minds of German airmen. According to the report in the newspaper for musicians and fans of popular music, the BBC planned a "Radio Dance Music Blitz on Germany".

RADIO DANCE MUSIC BLITZ ON GERMANY!

"Every afternoon at 4p.m., on 373 metres, a new form of Blitzkrieg descends on Germany. But it's not the RAF, which delivers it this time, only the best dance orchestras in Britain, presented with the acme of showmanship.

Wednesdays are the high spot. For then the programme is specially presented for the entertainment of the German Luftwaffe and on several occasions bands composed of RAF players have actually broadcast to their German counterparts! A week ago an RAF band with some famous players included in the personnel aired on this programme, and the show they gave has already resulted in a surprisingly large number of letters from listeners, all over the world – and some of them from Germany.

For the daily airings Geraldo has become almost the house band, although Ambrose, Mantovani and Jack Payne have already broadcast in the series. On Wednesdays it is the BBC policy to include as many of the RAF combinations as possible.

The entertainment angle in these programmes is definitely swing, with only a small proportion of sweet tunes thrown in to make up the balance. The success of the Wednesday afternoons has caused the BBC seriously to consider two special Luftwaffe airings each week, and a neutral journalist who recently arrived in this country after touring Germany and Occupied France is said to have told the officials of the Corporation that he actually heard the programme being received in the officers' mess at a German aerodrome!

Too much credit has been given to Dr. Joe Goebbels for his propaganda. We, for our part, tip our hats to the BBC for its realisation of the persuasive powers of really good dance music put over with imagination and skill for the cause of Britain."

Jack Payne, Henry Hall and Jack Hylton, three of the most popular bandleaders during the war.

Children queue for an impromptu daytime film show in London during the Blitz.

A blacked-out café in Rotherham, Yorkshire.

Charity Begins at Home

Throughout the conflict, singers, actors and comedians helped to raise money for all kinds of schemes to help the war effort. The star singer Frances Day did her bit in October 1940 by teaming up with Odeon Cinemas to raise money for the troops. She had more reason than many to support the war effort, having been born in America in 1908 as Frances Victoria Schenk, the daughter of artist Frank Schenk, of German-Jewish descent. She came to Britain in the late 1920s, married and lost all trace of her accent, having been given elocution lessons by her husband, the impresario Beaumont Alexander.

Tommy Trinder and the girls do an open air turn in Leicester Square in aid of Wings for Victory week in 1943.

Frances Day at the Odeon, Kingston, 2 October 1940.

Shortly after these pictures were taken Frances Day got engaged, having divorced Alexander, to an RAF pilot. He was later killed and there began a slow decline for the star who counted politicians and princes as her lovers. She died, a recluse, and in denial of her past in 1984.

Tommy Trinder took part in one of the regular wartime fundraising events to collect money in order to pay for aircraft. These went on across the country with counties, cities and towns endeavouring to outperform one another.

Professional actors serving at "a south-east coastal town" stage a show to raise money for homeless Londoners in October 1940.

Peace Offering

By May 1941 the huge threat of an invasion, Britain had abated but, extraordinarily, on the night of 10 May 1941 one German mounted a single-handed raid; he chose Scotland as the starting place. But why did 44-year-old Rudolph Hess fly to Britain? He was Hitler's deputy in the Nazi Party, which made it all the more incredible that he should take it upon himself to try to negotiate a peace that no one in the German High Command wanted. He parachuted to earth in South Lanarkshire, Scotland, before his aircraft crash-landed.

"I went out to get a weapon and the first thing I picked up was a hayfork. The parachute had reached the ground about 50 yards from our back door, and the airman was on the ground. I went up to him cautiously but he said that he had no weapon. The airman had hurt his leg, and was trying to get out of his parachute harness. I helped him to the cottage, and my mother, who was standing at the door, helped him in. We put him in an armchair. And he kept on thanking us for our goodness. My mother made tea, but he declined it, saying that he did not drink tea so late at night, but would enjoy a glass of water." – **David McLean**

For the Government Hess's arrival raised the potential of a propaganda coup and the BBC's German service were set to work on maximizing the opportunity almost immediately. Up to 10 times each day they carried reports detailing Hess's arrival.

The *Daily Mirror* was none too keen on reporting the event, however:

"We hope that those delusionists in this country who have a sneaking liking for Nazi ruffians in kid gloves will not lose their heads over Rudolf Hess. 'Welcome to our Blitzed country, liebe Herr Rudolf. So all is not well with the holy Fuehrer, no? We tell

The remains of Hess's aircraft guarded by police and soldiers.

you everything. You on our side now, yes? Have some tea. Take a cocktail. Join the Ministry of Information.'

Please, none of that!

Most illustrious — so far — of untrustworthy refugees this man Hess is only a little less criminal than those amongst his fellow-gangsters who boasted of their crimes. Hitler's deputy, Hitler's ersatz dictator, Hitler's shadow — Stellvertreter as the Germans call them — Rudolf Hess has condoned and abetted every villainy of National Socialism since he helped to compose the semi-literate Fuehrer's muddled Koran, 'Mein Kampf'. And now it seems that he is, amongst other nasty things, a skunk."

Of course nothing came of either Hess's flight to Britain, or of the BBC's German service's propaganda. Rudolf Hess was called insane by Hitler and the German propaganda machine; not that this prevented him from

being tried for war crimes at Nuremberg. Hess was sentenced to life imprisonment, which literally meant what it said. Rudolf Hess committed suicide in Berlin's Spandau Jail aged 92 in 1987.

Conspiracy theorists have said Hess came to Britian as a result of an MI5 invitation, although papers recently released seem to have put an end to that particular notion. However, others have tried to implicate the Duke of Kent, who died in a plane crash in Scotland during the war, as well as the King and Queen, in some kind of Machiavellian plot.

News Review, **which described itself as "the First British Newsmagazine", devoted three pages of its 22 May edition to Hess's arrival in Britain. It confirmed that Ivone Kirkpatrick, who had known Hess from his period of service at the British Embassy in Berlin, flew to Glasgow to confirm the German's identity.**

David McLean the Scottish ploughman who found Hess poses alongside his mother.

WAAFs take a break from their training to draw in a life study art class.

Suits You!

On 1 June, a few days after the sinking of the German battleship the *Bismarck* there was news on the home front that had a far greater, and more personnel, effect on everyone in Britain; the bad news was spelt out on the radio by Oliver Lyttleton, President of the Board of Trade.

"I want to talk to you this morning about clothes and boots and shoes. I have today made an order, which starts rationing these things, and you will see the details in the morning's newspapers. Coupons will now have to be given up when buying clothing in just the same way as when buying food. Everyone will have 66 clothing coupons to last them for 12 months. The first 26 coupons are in your present ration book. We all know that children grow out of their clothes, therefore they will be given more for their coupons than grown up people… I know everyone in these islands is prepared to undergo inconveniences and hardships if they are convinced of two things – that it is necessary and that it is fair. I want to assure you that the rationing of clothing is both."

Lyttleton went on to explain what the allowance would buy, and the paper rapidly got to work telling both men and woman how their wardrobe could be enlarged in any one year. "26 COUPONS FOR MAN'S SUIT" announced one headline. In broad terms 11 coupons were required for a new woollen dress, while a pair of man's trousers or a shirt were eight, and a pair of stockings, two and socks three. All in all it meant that a woman could buy two

RATIONING
of Clothing, Cloth, & Footwear *from June 1*

When the shops re-open you will be able to buy cloth, clothes, footwear and knitting wool *only if you bring your Food Ration Book with you*. The shopkeeper will detach the required number of coupons from the unused margarine page. Each margarine coupon counts as one coupon towards the purchase of clothing or footwear. You will have a total of 66 coupons to last you for a year; so go sparingly.

Remember you can buy *where* you like and *when* you like without registering.

NUMBER OF COUPONS NEEDED

MEN and BOYS	Adult	Child
Unlined mackintosh or cape	9	7
Other mackintoshes, or raincoat, or overcoat	16	11
Coat, or jacket, or blazer or like garment	13	8
Waistcoat, or pull-over, or cardigan, or jersey	5	3
Trousers (other than fustian or corduroy)	8	6
Fustian or corduroy trousers	5	5
Shorts	3	2
Overalls, or dungarees or like garment	6	4
Dressing-gown or bathing-gown	8	6
Night-shirt or pair of pyjamas	8	6
Shirt, or combinations—woollen	8	6
Shirt, or combinations—other material	5	4
Pants, or vest, or bathing costume, or child's blouse	4	2
Pair of socks or stockings	3	1
Collar, or tie, or pair of cuffs	1	1
Two handkerchiefs	1	1
Scarf, or pair of gloves or mittens	2	2
Pair of slippers or goloshes	4	2
Pair of boots or shoes	7	3
Pair of leggings, gaiters or spats	3	2

WOMEN and GIRLS	Adult	Child
Lined mackintoshes, or coats (over 28 in. long)	14	11
Jacket, or short coat (under 28 in. long)	11	8
Dress, or gown, or frock—woollen	11	8
Dress, or gown, or frock—other material	7	5
Gym tunic, or girl's skirt with bodice	8	6
Blouse, or sports shirt, or cardigan, or jumper	5	3
Skirt, or divided skirt	7	5
Overalls, or dungarees or like garment	6	4
Apron, or pinafore	3	2
Pyjamas	8	6
Nightdress	6	5
Petticoat, or slip, or combination, or cami-knickers	4	3
Other undergarments, including corsets	3	2
Pair of stockings	2	1
Pair of socks (ankle length)	1	1
Collar, or tie, or pair of cuffs	1	1
Two handkerchiefs	1	1
Scarf, or pair of gloves or mittens, or muff	2	2
Pair of slippers, boots or shoes	5	3

CLOTH. Coupons needed per yard depend on the width. For example, a yard of woollen cloth 36 inches wide requires 3 coupons. The same amount of cotton or other cloth needs 2 coupons.

KNITTING WOOL 1 coupon for two ounces

Extra coupons for bombed persons
Those who receive advances of money from the Assistance Board or the Department of Customs and Excise to enable them to replace clothing or footwear will receive at the same time extra coupons.

Goods by Post
If you are ordering goods by post you must cut out the proper number of coupons yourself, sign your name on the back and send them with the order. Otherwise coupons must be detached only by the shopkeeper.

THESE GOODS MAY BE BOUGHT *WITHOUT* COUPONS

¶ Children's clothing, of sizes generally suitable for infants less than 4 years old. ¶ Boiler suits and workmen's bib and brace overalls. ¶ Hats and caps. ¶ Sewing thread. ¶ Mending wool and mending silk. ¶ Boot and shoe laces. ¶ Tapes, braids, ribbons and other fabrics of 3 inches or less in width. ¶ Elastic. ¶ Lace and lace net. ¶ Sanitary towels. ¶ Braces, suspenders and garters. ¶ Hard haberdashery. ¶ Clogs ¶ Black-out cloth dyed black. ¶ All second-hand articles.

ISSUED BY THE BOARD OF TRADE

Woman modelling the latest utility fashion dress.

dresses; one woollen and one silk for 18 coupons, a skirt and a jumper for a further 12 coupons, a pair of pyjamas, and still have 28 left for a year's supply of underclothes, stockings and shoes.

As with any kind of system there were those that found ways around it. It was reported that in the first year of the scheme nearly 800,000 people claimed to have lost their ration books and were issued with new ones. It has even been claimed that some people adopted duel identities to get extra rations; though this was more common among those who wanted extra to eat. Black-marketers found all sorts of ways to profit from rationing – and of course there was no shortage of customers. Such were the puzzles associated with rationing that the paper was full of articles explaining the complexities of the Board of Trade's system.

Mrs Vera Killick modelling an embodied battledress tunic inspired by the make-do-and-mend philosophy.

A "No Coupon" sale taking place in a bombed out shop in Oxford Street, London, on 26 June 1941.

'Conchies'

When conscription was introduced in 1916 during the First World War there was enshrined in the Military Service Act of 1916 a right to "conscientious objection". Those who exercised this right could either perform civilian service or serve as a non-combatant in the army.

Objectors were required to convince a Military Service Tribunal of their status. In the Second World War around 60,000 people registered as conscientious objectors, and whereas in the First World War the tribunals were harsh in their assessments, there was now much greater leniency towards people who objected to "warfare as a means of settling international disputes". Some 3,000 were given complete exemption while around a third were dismissed as false claimants. Of those who registered 7,000 men were allocated to the Non-Combatant Corps, which placed men in companies responsible for clothing and food stores, in transport, or any military activity that did not require a man to handle "material of an aggressive nature".

Nearly 500 Non-Combatant Corps members worked in bomb disposal while others joined the ambulance service, fire service or joined the Merchant Navy. Around 5,500 were charged with offences relating to their unrecognized objection and sent to prison. Interestingly, according to a report in the *Mirror* during February 1940 Scotsmen were least likely to be "Conchies" as they were called; the Welsh most likely. There was a considerable stigma attached to being a CO; whatever a person's motives, many were labelled as cowards.

In July the *Daily Mirror* carried this story on the front page:

"A conscientious objector who was granted total exemption from military service joined the Merchant Navy – and died a hero. He was Arnold Baker of Bolton, Lancs, and tribute was paid to him yesterday at Manchester conscientious objectors tribunal. When Baker was given exemption there in 1939 Judge Burgis said that the tribunal was satisfied he would pull his weight. The chief officer of Baker's ship wrote saying that Baker

Conscientious objectors on their way to plead their case at Liverpool tribunal in 1941.

showed 'wonderful courage and bearing in the face of death without a thought for himself'. He voluntarily took over the wheel under heavy fire, with only the briefest instruction. When the steering was wrecked he asked to be given something else to do instead of making for his boat. 'He entirely fulfilled his promise to pull his weight, and died a wonderful example of British courage and bravery' the officer wrote. Judge Burgis said Baker's conduct was the clearest justification of the privilege granted to conscientious objectors.

Pearl Harbor

On 7 December 1941 radio stations across America broke into their regular programming with urgent announcements. "We interrupt this programme to bring you a special news bulletin. The Japanese have attacked Pearl Harbor, Hawaii, by air, President Roosevelt has just announced. The attack was also made on all naval and military activities on the principal island of Oahu."

In London the first news of the attacks was on the BBC's 9 o'clock news. Alvar Lidell told the nation that "Japan's long threatened aggression in the Far East began tonight with air attacks on the United States naval bases in the Pacific. Fresh reports are coming in every minute. Messages from Tokyo say the Japanese have announced a formal declaration of war against the United States and Britain." The following day both Houses of Parliament were recalled, and while it was obvious that America's involvement in the war would strengthen Britain's position this development would see the war

spread to other parts of the world, including the country's colonies, particularly those in the Far East.

As Churchill told Parliament: "We have at least four-fifths of the population of the globe upon our side. We are responsible for their safety – we are responsible for their future. In the past we had a light which flickered, in the present we have a light which flames, and in the future there will be a light which will shine calm and resplendent over all the land and all the sea!"

The First American Casualty. *With war undeclared, Japan attacked Pearl Harbour. American Isolationism died in the raid, as the United States lined up with Britain and Russia against the Axis.*

(December 8, 1941)

Three weeks before the attack on Pearl Harbor there was front-page news on the *Daily Mirror* of – NEWS IN NORTH ACCENT.

Mr Wilfred Pickles, who has " a North-country intonation which is unmistakable but not very pronounced," is to join the staff of BBC news announcers as an experiment. On the day after the attack Pickles read the 7 o'clock news.

"This is the BBC Home Service – Here is the news and this is Wilfred Pickles reading it. This morning's news of Japan's aggression is of successful counter-measures of invasion of Malaya. There have also been reports of enemy attacks on Thailand and Hong Kong..."

Pickles, a 37-year-old Yorkshireman, had been born in Halifax and in truth his "news-reading" accent was barely different from the standard BBC English of his colleagues. He seems to have slightly softened his speech pattern for news reading and to some extent his reputation as "the first of the many" has been somewhat exaggerated. He did though become something of an overnight sensation by ending his broadcasts with a "and to all in the North – Good-neet". By the end of the war Pickles was a radio celebrity and his series, *Have A Go*, proved so popular that it ran for around 20 years and regularly attracted audiences of over 15 million.

WILFRED PICKLES

Wartime Christmas

By the third Christmas of the war, having gone through the Blitz, the escalating fighting in the North African desert and the spreading conflict in the Far East, it was getting increasingly difficult to summon up good cheer and the means to celebrate. However, as they did throughout the war, people found the resolve, if only for the sake of the children.

The Gypsies of Abbey Wood needed paper for flower-making but as this was in short supply they used dyed woodshavings which they attached to the stalks, ready to be sold at Christmas.

A mother at home with her children hanging up the Christmas decorations.

Men on leave from HMS *Anson* give a Christmas party for the pupils of the Cranbrook Terrace School, Bethnal Green.

A railway guard decorating a Christmas tree at Holborn tube station.

Boys and girls evacuated from London to Itchingfield, Sussex, plucking poultry ready for Christmas.

Boatman, Old Alick, delivers the holly-topped boxes of Christmas gifts from the families ashore to the Rattray Head lighthouse keepers.

1942-1943
The long years

By 1942 Britain had been at war for over two years, and for almost a year bombing raids had been a regular nightly feature in many cities. It was a strain on everyone's nerves and made life unbearable for the hundreds of thousands who were "bombed out" of their homes. For these middle two years of the war there was little to cheer about. America's entry into the war also meant Britain was now fighting in the Far East against Japan, whose Imperial Army seemed unstoppable – for a while. People waited for news of loved ones who were abroad fighting, while doing their best to get on and make life as normal as possible.

"We shall not fail now. Let us move forward steadfastly together into the storm and through the storm." –Winston Churchill, 15 February 1942

People queuing in 1943 for horsemeat, which was not rationed during the war.

7 January	Relief of Leningrad launched
15 February	Surrender of Singapore to Japan
9 March	Surrender of Dutch East Indies to Japan
28 March	RAF bomb Lübeck
7 April	2,000 aircraft raid Malta
18 April	First USAAF raid on Japan
24 April	Luftwaffe begin the Baedeker raids on historic English cities; Exeter is first
20 May	Allied troops withdraw from Burma
4–6 June	US Navy beat Japanese Navy at Battle of Midway
10 June	Decision taken that the RAF will bomb Germany by night, the USAAF by day
21 June	Tobruk falls to Germans
7 July	German North African advance halted at El Alamein
17 August	First American bombing raid on France (Rouen)
19 August	Attack against Stalingrad is launched
23 October	Start of the 2nd Battle of El Alamein
4 November	General Rommel falls back at El Alamein
12 November	Germans break through Stalingrad to the Volga River
12 November	Naval battles at Guadalcanal in the Pacific
23 November	Tobruk retaken by Allies
19 November	Soviet forces launch counter-offensive against Stalingrad
30 December	Naval Battle of Barents Sea has Germans withdrawing
16 January	First air raid on Berlin for over a year
18 January	Soviet forces relieve Leningrad
23 January	Allies take Tripoli
27 January	First American bombing raid on Germany
9 February	Guadalcanal in American hands
9 March	Rommel leaves North Africa on sick leave
6 May	Final Allied North African offensive begins
16 May	Dambusters Raid
May	A record 41 U-boats lost in the month leading to almost all of them being withdrawn for the North Atlantic
10 July	Allies land on Sicily
3 September	New Italian Government signs armistice
9 September	Allies land at Salerno and Taranto
10 September	Germans occupy Rome
27 September	Germans begin withdrawal from the Ukraine
1 October	US troops enter Naples
13 October	Italy declares war on Germany
6 November	Kiev is liberated

Wings for Victory display in Trafalgar Square, 23 March 1943, featuring a Lancaster bomber, which was the type used on the famous Dambusters Raid.

The Columbia Club (American red cross club) organized a hayride and picnic lunch as a celebration of American Independence Day in July 1943. A US soldier and British girlfriend do the jitterbug.

Overpaid, Overfed, Oversexed and Over Here

Who could comedian Tommy Trinder have been referring to? It was of course American GIs, who started to arrive in Britain from January 1942 onwards; by 1943 there were almost 800,000 of them at bases up and down the country. The first arrived in Belfast on 26 January; soon they were disembarking from ships, including the *Queen Elizabeth* and the *Queen Mary*, in the Bristol Channel, on Clydeside and in Liverpool. From their various ports of arrival they made their way to army and air force bases throughout Britain. Many of the US Army Air Force personnel were stationed in East Anglia as part of the mighty 8th Air Force that conducted the devastating daylight bombing raids against Germany. Naturally, many American aircrews flew across the Atlantic, but for every man on flying missions there were 100 plus ground personnel whose job it was to fix the planes, feed the flyers and do all the administration jobs in support of

Black American troops singing in church at Great Doddington, Northamptonshire in October 1942.

the aircrew – and they came over by sea. By the end of 1944 over 420,000 USAAF men were based in East Anglia. By May 1944 there were over 1 million US soldiers in Britain.

For many people in Britain this was the first time that they came face to face with a "Yank" as they were almost universally called. American troops were even given a special handbook detailing how to deal with British people they came into contact with. Among the many pieces of sage advice was "Don't criticize the food, beer or cigarettes. Remember they have been at war since 1939."

In response to the British taunt of Overpaid, Overfed, Oversexed and Over Here, the Americans came up with one of their own about the British – underpaid, undersexed and under Eisenhower.

Captain Bender of California celebrates with crew members of the US 8th Air Force after finishing his 25th operation in March 1944.

The Crimes of War

Since the Second World War came to an end there has grown up something of an urban myth concerning crime during the war. Some people would have us believe that Britain was a crime free zone during the war, yet nothing could be further from the truth. Perhaps it's because the number of police in England and Wales dropped from over 82,000 when war broke out to fewer than 60,000 by the war's end. The simple reason for this drop in numbers was that younger policemen were called up to fight. Even those policemen who stayed in the Force could not always be relied upon to turn up for work – sick leave doubled.

Reported crimes rose by almost 60% between 1939 and 1945 to almost 480,000 – well over 1,000 a day. Given the environment in which these statistics were being collected the consensus is that they are an underestimate. If you opened a newspaper during the war there was a good chance you would find a crime story. Just as in peacetime, there were crimes of every kind from murder to robbery, assault to fraud, but there were also crimes unique to war. Of these the one that generated the most venom among both the media and the general population was looting.

In November 1940 at the height of the Blitz the *Daily Mirror* was in no doubt about what to do.

HANG A LOOTER, AND STOP THIS FILTHY CRIME.

Fines and imprisonment have done nothing to stop the ghouls who rob even bodies lying in the ruins of little homes. Looting, in fact, is on the increase. There have been more than 450 cases in London alone during the past 10 weeks. Yesterday brought another crop. A war reserve policeman was found guilty of looting in a bombed London house. He had been stationed there as a guard—against looters. And the articles he took

Women drivers of the Salford Lancashire Force, serve cups of tea each morning and afternoon to the men on point duty in February 1942.

belonged to a woman killed by the bomb, which wrecked her home. He got five years' penal servitude.

The paper reported elsewhere that for the first time since the war began crime was on the increase and that looting accounted for a large part of the rise. Robbing the gas meters in houses was a particularly popular form of looting, with 3,000 cases by February 1941. Among the looters were those in a position of trust – including ARP personnel, Auxiliary Fire Service members and so on – but also a lot of kids and under-21s who, for whatever reason, had not been called up and got in on the crime act. Looting often attracted people with no criminal record who struck when an opportunity arose which they saw as too good to turn down.

As this letter to the paper shows, ordinary citizens found it both baffling and very irritating, their feelings bordering on disgust.

While the courts had initially been lenient on

> When our house was bombed a few weeks ago we had to leave it in the middle of the night. We returned as soon as possible and packed everything we could into one large room, until we could remove it. While we were away some dirty cad sneaked in and stole my daughter's doll's pram and a huge doll, which she treasured, besides taking our blankets and many other things. May Hitler favour that thief with a visit – soon – and pay him well for his trouble.

looters they got increasingly tough until, for example, six Auxiliary Fire Service officers received five years for stealing whisky that they drank on the spot.

Robbery

Looting became the new robbery for much of the war, although it did not totally wipe out the age-old practice of thieving.

In March 1941 a youth who went in for some robbery got the kind of treatment that would be unacceptable today.

Twenty strokes with the birch and three years Borstal was the sentence passed yesterday at the Old Bailey on a youth now 17 who laid in wait in a dark passage for men returning home with their wages, struck seven down with a wooden pickaxe shaft and robbed them. The youth, who was 16 at the time of the offences, is George Ernest Knapp, a Dagenham tiler, said to have been earning as much as £6 a week. Passing sentence, the Recorder, Sir Gerald Dodson, said: "after a long experience of criminal cases I can never recall such a case as this." Knapp pleaded guilty to four charges of robbery with violence, and asked for three offences of assault and attempted robbery to be taken into consideration.

Perhaps the most notorious robberies during the war were in early 1941 when a gang of safe breakers used the blackout as cover for their activities. They had a van painted to look like an ARP ambulance and got away with £20,000 (well over £2 million in today's money).

The nation's obsession with food or the lack of it was the reason some people were driven to crime, as was revealed by one story.

"Four men in a substantial position, but with no conception of honesty" as Mr Justice Staba described them, were each gaoled for three years yesterday for food racketeering. "I will show such men no mercy," said the Judge, sentencing them at Birmingham Assizes to penal servitude in a case concerning the theft of two tons of butter. "It was a deliberate carefully-planned robbery. That is bad enough in ordinary times. But now this country is in the position of a besieged fortress, with every man, woman and child in the front line, and one of the most vital spots the common enemy has been striking for two years is the food supply to the nation."

The men would have sold their haul on the black market. In 1941 the Government announced that people who held food stocks could be sent to prison. Petrol had become very desirable, especially after fuel for private motoring was banned during 1942. A favourite tactic of the police was to visit horse race meetings and question the race goers as to how they got to the course. While fake petrol coupons were popular those for clothing were even more sought after, in part because the number of privately owned cars when war broke out was still relatively small, whereas everyone had to clothe themselves.

Policemen standing outside the sandbagged entrance to their police station.

Evelyn Oatley, murder victim
No. 1 of the four women murdered by
Gordon Cummins.

Gordon Frederick Cummins, 28 - year - old RAF Cadet, most notorious killer since Jack the Ripper, who was sentenced to death at the Old Bailey for the murder of Evelyn Oatley, 35-year-old ex-revue actress. The Judge described it as a "sadistic sexual murder of a ghoulish type."
At the police-court hearing, he was said to have done to death four women and to have attempted to kill two others.

Murder Most Foul

Between 1939 and 1945, with all the killing as a result of the war, the actual number of murders actually dropped from pre-war levels. There were, however, some notable exceptions, particularly the man known as the "Blackout Ripper".

Gordon Frederick Cummins, a 28-year-old RAF cadet, most notorious killer since Jack the Ripper, was yesterday at the Old Bailey sentenced to the gallows. This handsome young murderer, whose strong, flexible, well-kept hands were alleged at the police court hearing to have done to death four women, and to have attempted to kill two others, received his sentence with a

calm which amazed the Court (gripping the front of the dock, he said in a cultured voice; "I am absolutely innocent").

Mr Justice Asquith had described the murder of Evelyn Oatley, 35-year-old ex-revue actress, as a "sadistic sexual murder of a ghoulish type". Cummins had used a safety-razor blade to hack at her throat until she died. And then as the last breath left her he used a tin opener to gash and mutilate her. This murder opened up five days of horror. Within a few days of the discovery of Evelyn Oatley's body in her Wardour Street flat, three other women had been strangled and murdered.

Faced with its biggest murder problem in more than 50 years, Scotland Yard packed the area with all available C.I.D. and uniformed men, under Chief Inspector Edward Greeno. Women decoys were employed to trap the murderer. And then on Friday 13 February, Cummins made a mistake. He left his respirator, bearing his name and Service Number – 525987 – in a Haymarket air raid shelter. There he had tried to claim another victim, but she screamed, and he ran away. She hurried to a police station, gasped out her story, and the respirator was found.

Next morning, a few minutes before reveille at his barracks, Cummins awoke to find his bed surrounded by police officers. He was unconcerned, and said the whole thing was ridiculous. But the evidence was too strong. Cummins is left-handed, and fingerprints of his left hand were found on Evelyn Oatley's mirror and on the tin opener. Gordon Cummins was a poseur.

He cultivated his accent and boasted of his connections with the aristocracy. His father is superintendent of an approved school for boys from whom he received frequent remittances. But this was not enough. He stole from the women he killed.

To the end his young wife had faith in her husband. Mrs Cummins is 28. They had been married five and a half years. There are no children. Cummins was born at New Eastwick, Yorkshire. He went to Llandoveris County School and moved with his father to Harlestone, Northampton where he attended Northampton Technical School, after leaving school he worked in the laboratory of a firm at Swiss Cottage London. He joined the RAF in November 1935 and had achieved his ambition to be accepted for training as a pilot.

This was the first murderer to be given the "Ripper" tag by the newspapers since the days of the infamous Jack the Ripper. Cummins, who was Britain's first serial killer of the 20th century, was hanged on 25 June 1942 at Wandsworth Prison.

A policeman comes to the aid of a lady and carries her to an ambulance in the heart of the City of London after an air raid.

179

One of several German guns captured by the 8th Army in Libya arriving in Woolwich as exhibits for the borough's Wings for Victory week in March 1943.

The Post Office at War

Amidst all the difficulties, raging from the Blitz to families being moved around the country following evacuation or simply having to move a few streets having been "bombed out", somehow the mail still got through. The 75,000 workers who left its employ to go to war exacerbated the problems for the post office. Many of these places were filled by women, who had the task of sorting the huge number of letters and parcels, many of which were sent abroad to a front line – somewhere in the world. In September 1940, during the early days of the Blitz, the *Daily Mirror* highlighted the issue of bombed out victims:

Scraps of paper pinned to the wrecked doorways of bombed homes show how out of date London street directories are these days. The notes tell postmen and tradesmen that Mrs Brown has moved to No. 17 in the next street, or

WHY YOU MUST

POST *much* EARLIER

THIS CHRISTMAS

LATEST POSTING DATE—DEC. 18—*but the sooner the better!*

Because you want to give your letter the best possible chance of arriving in time.

Because the Post Office has already released a very large number of its employees to the forces and cannot, this year, engage all its usual extra Christmas staff.

Because everything (from blackout to 'incidents') that holds up normal train and road services also holds up postal deliveries.

Because, in short, there's a war on.

WARTIME GIFT SUGGESTION.
Why not send War Savings Certificates or National Savings Gift Tokens. Buy them at any Post Office. They will save you and the postman trouble, give a lot of pleasure, and help to win the war. Of course, you can also send Postal Orders.

GPO

that Mr Jones wants his correspondence delivered to a district miles away.

Some postmen have been doing the re-delivery themselves when the new address has been on or near their round, but usually they make a note of the address and hand the letters back at the sorting office. The G.P.O. yesterday issued instructions, which will meet this

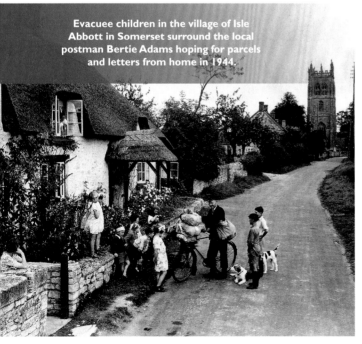

Evacuee children in the village of Isle Abbott in Somerset surround the local postman Bertie Adams hoping for parcels and letters from home in 1944.

problem and remove the danger of abuse of this unofficial delivery system. People, who remain temporarily near their old home after it has been made uninhabitable, should ask the local post office where they can collect their correspondence.

Those who move to other districts, leaving their former homes unoccupied, should apply at any post office for a redirection card as soon as they have a permanent address. The card, P.221G.B, has been specially produced for this emergency. It should be used also by people remaining in their original neighbourhood if they have taken up new quarters on a fairly permanent basis.

Strikes

Under regulations put in place at the outbreak of the war, strikes were illegal. Defence regulations called for maximum productivity from all manufacturers, suppliers and service industries to support the war effort, but making such regulations stick was easier said than done, not least because of the amount of time it would take to prosecute vast numbers of strikers and because it was not clear where to imprison them. By 1942 the number of working days lost through strikes had gone back to pre-war levels.

Women munitions workers using an army lorry during a bus strike in May 1943. Like so many strikes before and since, this one was over pay and conditions.

The strike at the shipbuilding yard in Barrow-in-Furness in October 1943 was over the bonus system to be paid. It was eventually resolved at a meeting at the local football ground attended by 6,000 workers who voted to go back to work.

Women on strike outside the Houses of Parliament in September 1942. Unfortunately no record exists as to why they were striking. On the day after this photograph was taken a woman in Luton in Bedfordshire was in court at the request of a committee of fellow workers. The machine minder's offence was described by the chairman of Luton magistrates as "a serious case of deliberate malingering". The woman had only worked for two and a half days since being taken on by the firm in May and a committee of five workers had recommended that an example be made of her by prosecution. She was sentenced to two months in prison.

POWs

In 1939, when very little fighting had actually taken place, there were just two prison of war camps in Britain. By the end of the war this number had soared to 600, and the camps were located in almost every area of Britain. Between 1940 and the middle of 1943, when there was still a threat of invasion, the British Government was unhappy about accepting large numbers of prisoners, for obvious reasons. A solution was found by sending many to camps in Canada.

German prisoners who were suspected of being strong Nazi sympathizers were sent to camps in remote parts of Britain, particularly the Scottish Highlands. German POWs were fed on the same food rations as British service personnel, but many suffered with various mental and stress related complaints as they received little word about their families or their country.

At the end of the war POWs were reviewed before being released to establish if there were any traces of loyalty to the Nazi cause. The first of the 400,000 prisoners held in Britain went back to Germany in 1946; the last ones were repatriated in November 1948.

Among some of the earliest POWs were these German airmen captured after an air raid in August 1940. It was probably six years before they saw their homes again.

While fraternization between British civilians and the POWs was strictly forbidden there were examples of a relaxing of the rules when war was over. At Christmas 1945 many British families chose to take POWs into their homes to enjoy Christmas together.

By the end of 1947, a quarter of a million POWs had been repatriated; of these 24,000 decided to stay in Britain. Among them was Bert Trautmann who went on to become Manchester City's much loved goalkeeping legend.

German soldiers in a POW camp in southwest Cornwall photographed in November 1945. They are making toys for free distribution at Christmas time to orphaned children of servicemen and children whose fathers had been disabled in the war.

It was not just German POWs that were held in Britain. These are Italian prisoners of war seen arriving at London's Waterloo railway station in May 1943.

Women at War

Two airmen who have just arrived from overseas being checked in by WAAF in November 1943.

In December 1941 Britain became the first country to conscript women; those between 20 and 30 were liable for military service. They could join the ATS (Auxiliary Territorial Service), the WRNS (Women's Royal Naval Service) or WAAF (Women's Auxiliary Air Force). They could also be put to work in the area of Civil Defence or in industry. Many women volunteered, and by the war's end over 120,000 had been "called up".

Interestingly, it was the WAAF and the WRNS who faired better in recruiting as most women found the uniforms appealing! In the early days of the war many women deserted, but given the fact that the only punishment was dismissal this may not have been much of

In March 1943 ATS women on a lonely gun position pass the hours between alarms by doing embroidery work.

a deterrent. Soon the women were subject to the same regulations as the soldiers, but this was also matched by a distinct improvement in their working conditions.

One area of the home defence that benefited from women was the Anti Aircraft Command. Desperately short of men, there was initial resistance to women being used but eventually the numbers game made this inevitable. However, the Government and those in charge of the Ack-Ack Batteries had to overcome many prejudices from the parents of young girls as well as practical difficulties that included mixed accommodation.

By 1943 there were over 180,000 serving WAAFs; their work ranged from catering to meteorology, transport, telegraphy, codes and ciphers, as well as working in Operation Rooms, as depicted in films of the Battle of Britain where they are seen directing the fighter pilots.

By the end of the war there were 190,000 members of the ATS and at its peak, in 1944, there were 75,000 WRNS.

London shopgirl attacks Nazis—

1. With the shop half empty and so little to sell, my old job began to seem pointless.

2. My boy is in the R.A.F.— so I went to train for work in making aeroplanes.

3. Soon I was passed to a factory, for a worthwhile job helping to make big bombers.

4. And Jim has just got his wings. Who knows? I might have worked on the plane he flies.

Is YOUR work really vital to the War Effort? Go to your local office of the Ministry of Labour and National Service and ask their advice. They will tell you how best to serve your country.

YOUR DUTY NOW IS WAR WORK

ISSUED BY THE MINISTRY OF LABOUR & NATIONAL SERVICE

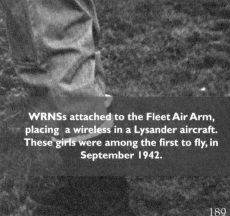

WRNSs attached to the Fleet Air Arm, placing a wireless in a Lysander aircraft. These girls were among the first to fly, in September 1942.

Women's Work – Civvy Street

Among the many photographs of women at work during the war are some that are posed and somewhat patronizing in the way women are presented. But there was no doubting the hard work that many women put in to support the war effort. For a number of men it was the sheer surprise of learning just how capable women were that caused this reaction.

Window cleaners in 1941

Delivering boxes of fish to traders in Billingsgate Market, London, in September 1943.

Operating a power hammer at the LNER railway works in May 1942.

Riveters at work at a Scottish shipyard in March 1942.

The production line of Hawker Hurricane aircraft in 1942.

YMCA mobile canteen in November 1940.

The Women for Westminster Movement

Despite, or possibly because of women getting increasingly involved in all aspects of the work place, things were beginning to change on the political scene. With no contested elections during the war, politics was relatively dormant, but some women were very unhappy with what they considered their under-representation in Parliament, and took action.

In February 1942 at their first meeting, the Movement announced that it wanted to get 100 women returned to Parliament at the first General Election after the war was over. They even organized a "school" at premises in Dartmouth Street, London SW1, at which they planned to teach women public speaking, how to mount an election campaign and publicity schemes.

By May the *Daily Mirror* was reporting,

The women's section of the Labour Party are asking for more women candidates to be accepted as possible post-war MPs. This feeling is growing and there has been established a women for Westminster movement.

They hold regular school meetings – where speeches are made, rude interruptions thrown at the speakers and not so polite answers given. The girls get together and have a mock election meeting, and take a vote on whether the speaker convinces them or not. The school will shortly be addressed by Edith Summerskill on Parliamentary procedure. This is a good idea, but I don't understand why women cannot go about it through their local parties. The best MPs are those who have worked for their party and done the hard ground work in the committee rooms and local government.

Women for Westminster Movement rally at Hyde Park Corner. The speaker had just asked the crowd to raise their hands for equal pay for men and women.

Edith Summerskill was a Labour MP for Fulham and became a minister in Clement Attlee's postwar Labour Government; at this time she was one of 21 women Labour MPs. This was followed by the Women for Westminster Movement holding a rally on Sunday 16 August 1942. Among those who addressed the meeting was 52-year-old Rebecca Sieff, the eldest daughter of Michael Marks, the founder of Marks & Spencer. She was married to Israel Sieff, who worked on the British Palestine Committee and in 1918 was a founding member and first president of the Federation of Women Zionists of Great Britain and Ireland. Another woman, Elaine Burton, finally became an MP in 1950 having failed at two previous attempts. Monica Whately was a prominent campaigner for women's rights and civil liberties.

elected to Parliament, which represented almost 4% of the total number of MPs. For the remaining 40 years this figure stayed around the same level. In 1987 it reached 41, by 1992 60 and in 1997 it reached 120. Today the number stands at 128, which represents 20% of the total number of MPs. It's still a long way off the dreamed of 50% that the Women in Westminster were advocating during the war.

This rally was not reported anywhere in the *Daily Mirror*, and all mention of the movement ended. That is until December 1944 when a small entry in the *Mirror* reported that "A Brains Trust, to be held at 6pm on December 28, and organised by the "Women for Westminster" movement. Women who have already been adopted as candidates for Parliament, by all the Parties, will answer the questions submitted." The title of the debate was "A Woman's place she just became an MP is in the home."

Over the coming months news of local branches of the Women for Westminster Movement appeared in the *Daily Mirror*. In Liverpool its members demanded that women be appointed to the housing committee of the local council.

In the 1945 General Election a total of 24 women were

A tennis competition in London involving staff from the Japanese Embassy who were living under house arrest, but were allowed out accompanied by police guards. They are seen here playing tennis in London on 7 May 1942, two months before being repatriated.

The Enemy in London

Following the declaration of war between Britain and Japan the enemy literally was at the gates of London.

The staff of the Japanese Embassy and Consulate were effectively interned, under heavy guard, and lived at three London addresses – the Chancellery, in Prince's Gate, Portman Square, and Grosvenor Square (where the Japanese Ambassador resided, in the large corner house).

In March 1942 the *Daily Mirror* printed a picture of Japanese diplomats smiling and laughing, while out for

Most Japanese left London as relations grew increasingly strained between Britain and Japan over Japanese support for Germany. This family is seen leaving Euston station in June 1940 to return home to Japan.

a walk in London with a police escort. The paper was none too pleased given the news that was filtering back from the Far East of what some Japanese forces were reported to have done to British troops.

In July the *Daily Mirror* announced that, "When 1,800 British and Allied Nationals at present, in Japanese hands reach the Portuguese East African port of Lourenço Marques, they will be exchanged for Japanese diplomats and civilian internees. The exchange, which will take place on August 27 and September 7 has been arranged through the Swiss Government. The British and Allied party consists of about 550 British and 200 Allied officials, with their wives, families, and dependents, 840 British non-officials, and 210 Allied non-officials."

On the day the picture of Japanese Embassy staff playing tennis appeared in the *Daily Mirror* this was the front page.

Invasion!

While the immediate threat of invasion under which the country lived during the summer of 1940 and on into 1941 had receded the German Army and Luftwaffe were still just across the English Channel, so the danger was ever present. Just as British, Canadian and American commandos had raided Dieppe in August 1942, the Germans could do something similar.

On 25 October 1942 the *Daily Mirror*'s former star photographer, Bernard Alfieri, spent the day in Kingston-on-Thames photographing an invasion exercise. None of the photographs he took that day appeared in the newspaper at the time. They serve as both a reminder of what Britain lived under during those long middle years of the war, as well as a testament to those on the home front.

Home Guard and Ambulance Services.

Civil Defence wardens mixing up disinfectant.

1944-1945
And in the end

"The prevailing emotion of 1944 is best described by the words forward looking." This is how Winston Churchill described the situation at the start of 1944. There was a growing feeling of wanting it all to be over. Although Churchill had warned everyone that the war was likely to be long, the strain of living under such circumstances increased from year to year. By the time of the Normandy landings in June 1944 there was a sense that it could not last much longer. However, the powerful German Army, despite having been depleted from its attritional war on the Russian front, was putting up stiff resistance, and it was to be another 11 months before the fighting in Europe finished – 11 months in which the terror of German rocket attacks on Britain brought the return of war to the home front.

"*Four years ago our nation and Empire stood alone against an overwhelming enemy, with our backs to the wall. Tested as never before in our history, in God's Providence we survived that test. The spirit of the people, resolute, dedicated, burned like a bright flame lit surely, from those unseen fires, which nothing can quench.*" **– King George VI, 6 June 1944**

A sailor from Cambridge being welcomed home in May 1945 after three years three months as a prisoner of war at Marlag M.

1944

22 January •	Allies land at Anzio
27 January •	Leningrad relieved after an almost 800-day siege
5 June •	US Army enters Rome
6 June •	D-Day
13 June •	V-1 rockets fired against Britain
19 June •	Battle of Philippines Sea; Japan loses 400 aircraft
20 July •	Unsuccessful attempt on Hitler's life by German officers
15 August •	Allies land in southern France
25 August •	Allies enter Paris
2 September •	Brussels liberated
8 September •	V-2 rockets fired against Britain
14 September •	Russians enter Warsaw
29 September •	First B.29 raid on Japanese mainland
12 October •	Germans leave Athens

1945

13 January •	Russia begins advance into East Prussia
17 January •	Warsaw falls
10 February •	First US air raids on Tokyo
13 February •	Allies bomb Dresden
1 March •	US Army seizes bridge across the Rhine
22 March •	Allies under Patton cross the Rhine
1 April •	US forces land on Okinawa
11 April •	Allies take Hannover
14 April •	Russians take Vienna
20 April •	Allies capture Nuremberg
26 April •	First Russian shells hit Hitler's chancellery in Berlin
28 April •	Mussolini killed by Italian partisans
30 April •	Hitler commits suicide
2 May •	Berlin surrenders
8 May •	VE Day: Germany signs surrender at midnight
11 May •	Last German troops surrender to Russians in Czechoslovakia
5 July •	British General Election
6 August •	Atomic bomb dropped on Hiroshima
9 August •	Atomic bomb dropped on Nagasaki
15 August •	Emperor Hirohito broadcasts surrender
2 September •	Japan formally surrenders

P.38 Lightning aircraft used by the United States Army Air Force for long-range bomber protection, waiting to be assembled at a base in England in February 1944.

Lifeboat Men

Many younger lifeboat crewmen either volunteered for the services or were called up during the war, which raised the average age of crewmen to 50 years old; some as old as 70 served in this vital role. Many of the lifeboat crews were also fishermen, so they performed two important roles; the men at Lindisfarne on Holy Island in Northumberland also doubled as a Home Guard unit.

At Dunkirk in 1940, 19 lifeboats went across to pick up survivors off the beaches, and only one craft, the *Viscountess Wakefield* from Hythe, was lost. Besides their normal role of rescuing civilians from sunken craft, whether through enemy action or natural disasters, the lifeboats rescued many downed airmen, especially from the North Sea.

Henry Blogg, coxswain of the Cromer lifeboat, is affectionately known as the "greatest of all lifeboat men"; he was already 63 when the war started. During

By January 1944 the lifeboat men of Sheringham, Norfolk, held the record for the number of airmen's lives saved from the North Sea – 27 had so far been rescued.

his career he was awarded three RNLI Gold Medals, four Silver Medals, the George Cross and the British Empire Medal. His last award was a Silver Medal won in 1941 when he and his crew went to the rescue of the stricken merchantman MV *English Trader*. On its way to the

Women of Runswick Bay in Yorkshire, launching the lifeboat.

floundering ship the Cromer lifeboat, *H F Bailey*, rolled on to its side throwing five of the men overboard, including Blogg. All the men were recovered after the lifeboat righted itself, but one of them died back on board. Blogg headed for the nearest port, Great Yarmouth, but at 3am the next morning he roused his crew and they headed off to the stricken vessel because the 47 crew were not expected to last until morning. Blogg and his crew rescued all the men, for which he won the last of his silver medals.

The lifeboat man who died was named Edward Allen; of the 12 crewmen only he, Blogg and Sidney Harrison did not have the surname Davies. This shows how remarkably close-knit were the communities that these men came from. Henry "Shrimp" Davies took over as coxswain from his uncle, Henry Blogg, in 1947 and served in the position until 1976 when he carried on running the family deckchair business on Cromer's East Beach.

Lifeboat men of Sheringham, Norfolk, stand by during operational flights over the North Sea to rescue airmen who may have dropped into the sea in January 1944.

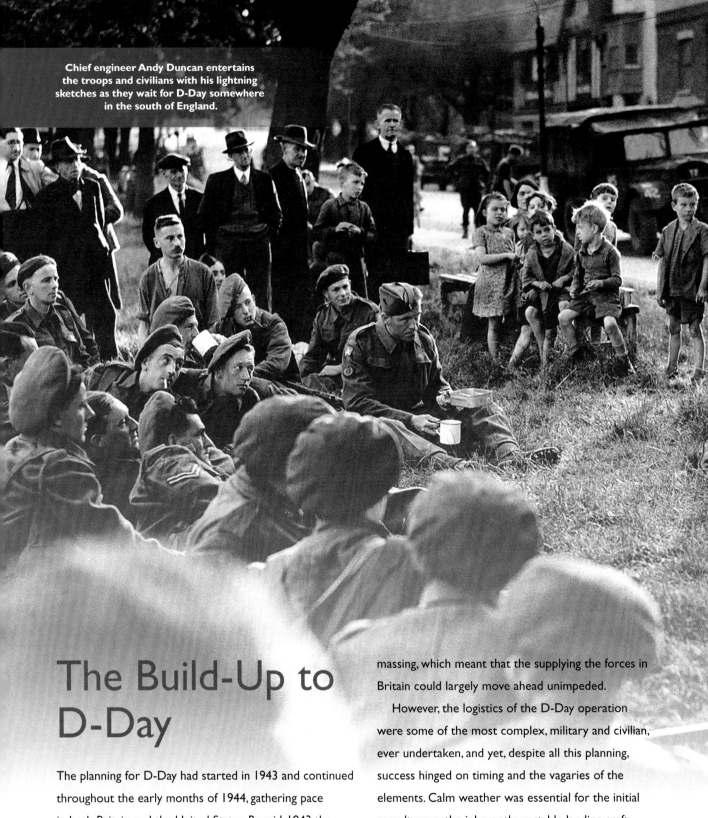

Chief engineer Andy Duncan entertains the troops and civilians with his lightning sketches as they wait for D-Day somewhere in the south of England.

The Build-Up to D-Day

The planning for D-Day had started in 1943 and continued throughout the early months of 1944, gathering pace in both Britain and the United States. By mid-1943 the U-boat menace to merchant shipping in the Atlantic had largely disappeared thanks to effective air patrols and, most importantly, the deciphering of German Enigma codes that gave warnings of where the U-boats were

massing, which meant that the supplying the forces in Britain could largely move ahead unimpeded.

However, the logistics of the D-Day operation were some of the most complex, military and civilian, ever undertaken, and yet, despite all this planning, success hinged on timing and the vagaries of the elements. Calm weather was essential for the initial assault wave; the inherently unstable landing craft needed relatively smooth seas to be able to deliver their cargoes of men and machines onto the French beaches. A low spring tide was also vital to expose the German beach defences; the troops also needed

General Bernard Montgomery stands on the bonnet of a jeep on 21 May 1944 as he addresses the troops during a pre D-Day inspection tour.

10-year-old Edna McCundle entertains the troops just before the D-Day landings.

a clear half moon for the massive parachute drops.

Shortly before D-Day some 1.5 million US service personnel had arrived in the UK – around 700,000 of those in the first six months of 1944. They were scattered in bases across Britain, many in camps stretching across the whole of the south of England. The British Army had by this time reached almost 3 million men, with many Commonwealth troops in Britain (including 250,000 Canadians) as well as men from France, Poland, Holland and other countries in Europe conquered by the Nazis.

Britain in early 1944 looked like a huge military training ground.

D-Day

"This is London, London calling in the Home Overseas and European Services and through United Nations Radio Mediterranean, and this is John Snagge speaking. Supreme Headquarters Allied Expeditionary Force have just issued Communiqué No. 1. Under the command of General Eisenhower, Allied naval forces, supported by strong air forces, began landing Allied armies this morning on the northern coast of France. I'll repeat that communiqué…"

– John Snagge, BBC Home Service, 9.32am, 6 June 1944

The announcement was hardly news, just an official confirmation of what many

For **D-Day** people in **East Ham** worked together to provide a worthwhile send-off for troops passing through their district to embark for France. Money was raised to provide cigarettes, drinks and food, while some people even contributed their week's rations.

people had heard during the evening and night of 5/6 June when thousands of sorties were flown by the RAF and the USAAF. As well as hearing the roar of the bombers overhead, those in the south of England witnessed the constant flow of traffic heading towards the coast to act as the second, and subsequent waves of troops set to cross the Channel and support the invasion. The operation should have begun a day earlier but bad weather had delayed things by 24 hours.

A crowd distributes food and drink to troops.

A newspaper seller had to ration the first edition to regular customers only.

D-Day in Numbers

1 – Victoria Cross awarded during the landings to Company Sergeant Major Stanley Hollis

1.30am – the parachute landings begin

6.30am – the landings begin.

50 – mile stretch of Normandy coast on which the landings took place

4,126 – transport and landing craft

4,300 – British and Canadian casualties

6,000 – American casualties

6,939 – ships involved in the landings

11,680 – aircraft deployed

14,674 – aircraft sorties were flown on D-Day

29,000 – airborne troops

31,000 – the number of airmen involved in the operation

61,715 – British troops as a part of the 2nd Army Group

73,000 – American troops in the First Army contingent

83,115 – the 2nd Army contingent

156,115 – troops landed on D-Day

The 1st Battalion, South Lancashire Regiment, together with elements of the Middlesex Regiment make their way up Sword beach from their landing craft on D-Day.

D-Day
Aftermath

British troops in Sherman tanks roll through the narrow cobbled streets of a Normandy town, July 1944.

A British Army DUKW passes through the Normandy village of Courseulles during the push towards Caen.

Civilians evacuated from the Normandy invasion area arriving at Waterloo station in London on 13 June.

Airmen who may be waiting to join their comrades on the Continent study a map of France in a London bookshop.

Lorries and jeeps driving off the Mulberry harbour at Gold Beach, Arromanches. A Mulberry was a prefabricated harbour.

These officers and men are all that are left from four German divisions after the capture of Cherbourg.

Robot Planes and Rockets

"There will be many false alarms, many feints, many dress rehearsals. We may also ourselves be the objects of new forms of attack from the enemy. Britain can take it." **– Winston Churchill**

In late March 1944 Churchill gave a speech in which he made this passing reference to what might happen in the near future. It was a prediction that unfortunately was to become all too true. A week after the D-Day landings men on duty at a Royal Observer Corps station in Kent's Romney Marshes saw a strange glowing black object in the sky heading towards them – they were baffled, having never seen anything like it before. It was a sight that was to become all too familiar, as it was the first V-1 rocket, one of 10 pilotless "aircraft" fired from launch sites in France that day. On this first occasion only four made it across the Channel, and only one reached London, where it crash-landed in Grove Road in Hackney killing six people. It was the start of the shorter, but no less frightening Blitz.

Prime Minister Winston Churchill at Tufton Street, Westminster, at an incident caused by a 'robot plane' as the *Daily Mirror* described it in June 1944.

The first confirmation for most of Britain of this new aerial threat appeared in the *Daily Mirror* on Saturday 17 June. Given the potential threat, and against a background of the Normandy landings, the need to maintain domestic morale was the overriding consideration for the government. It was one of those situations where the news needed to be managed and the extent of the threat examined before saying too much, too soon. Initially some sections of the press called them "robot machines", which somehow made them sound even more sinister. Herbert Morrison, the Home Secretary, made a more measured statement:

"The enemy has begun to use his secret weapon – the pilotless aircraft. The damage it has caused has been relatively small, and the new weapon will not interfere with our war effort and our sure and steady march to victory. The enemy's aim is clearly, in view of the difficulty of his military situation, to try to upset our morale and interfere with our work. It is essential that there should be the least possible interruption in all work vital to the country's needs at this time, and the Government's counsel is that everyone should get on with his or her job in the ordinary way and only take cover when danger is imminent."

Four days later and they had been christened "DoodleBugs" and "buzz-bombs", which made them seem less threatening, although it did nothing to reduce their effectiveness. By the end of June around 80 V-1s were hitting the London area every day, on some days over 120 would reach their target; one hit the Air Ministry in the Aldwych and killed almost 50 people.

Who You Gonna Call? Robot-Busters

The RAF was once again at the forefront of Britain's defence, fighting what was almost a mini Battle of Britain, or the "Doodlebug Summer" as some named it. Given the requirement to support the land forces in France, as well as the many other theatres of war, it was a major challenge to combat the doodlebugs, but a vital one given the threat to the civilian population, and particularly those living in the southeast. Such was the threat to morale that

Churchill personally ordered that the RAF would fly in any and all weathers in order to reinforce the will of the people on the ground. He deduced that it was important for civilians to hear the sound of the RAF defending them. The first report of the RAF's battle with the V-1s was on the front page of the *Daily Mirror* on 22 June.

Top scorer in the battle is Flight-Lieutenant A R Moore. Five crosses followed his name on his squadron's notice board yesterday. Slim, and modest, with his hair blowing about his head and a smudge of oil on his cheek, he told the Daily Mirror of his latest kill.

"It was about 8 o'clock this morning I got it. It was about 30 miles out and it went down. The bomb went off in the sea. All

A Hawker Typhoon squadron with its maintenance crew on a tea break. The Hawker Tempest was a faster derivative of the Typhoon.

he left behind was a towering water spout. Two of his 'kills' blew up in mid-air. The last time one blew up, I turned over," he added laconically.

Competition for the position as leading robot buster is keen in the fighter squadrons that have many kills to their credit. Flying the RAF's new wonder fighter, the Tempest, fastest aircraft in service, these pioneers of the Battle of the Robots have evolved their own technique from scratch.

Leader of the Buzz bomb beaters is Wing-Commander R P Beamont, DSO double DFC (Buzz bomb score: Three).

"When we attack them in daylight we have to look for them against the sky and then make a climbing attack," he said. "At first we attacked from a range of 400 yards, but now we find it is quite safe to fire at them from even 100 yards. They usually blow up, but hits from the Tempest's cannon will often knock bits off them and upset the gyro, and then the robot crashes. Sometimes when the gyro has been damaged they will do the most wonderful aerobatics all over the sky before crashing. When you make your attack, it is like firing at a large flame with wings sprouting from it. Your cannon scores hits and suddenly there is a big red flash and you find your plane covered with blazing oil. There is a terrific jerk and you often find your-self coining through upside down."

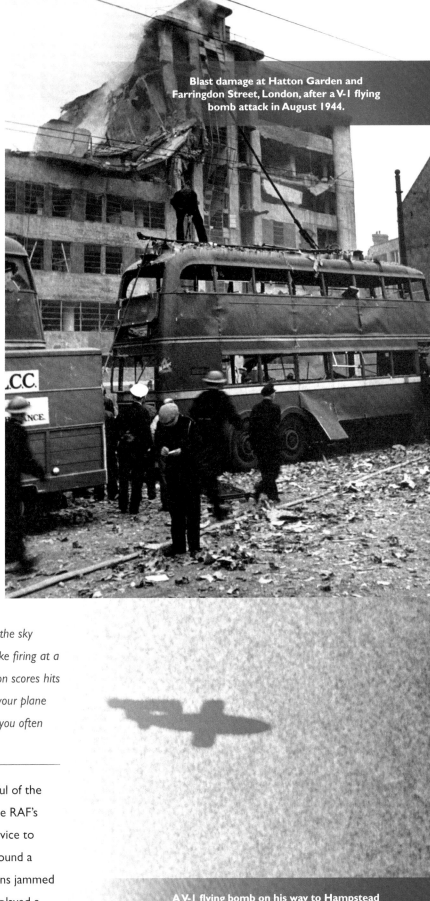

Blast damage at Hatton Garden and Farringdon Street, London, after a V-1 flying bomb attack in August 1944.

A V-1 flying bomb on his way to Hampstead in June 1944.

The Hawker Tempest was the most successful of the RAF's planes and shot down almost 700 V-Is. The RAF's first jet fighter, the Meteor, was rushed into service to counter the menace, but only accounted for around a dozen kills; its speed wasn't the issue, but its guns jammed all too regularly. The anti-aircraft batteries also played a valuable part in countering the menace.

Normal Life. . .

By the time the Doodlebug summer came along there had been five years of war on the home front and people had reached a point where they thought that the likelihood of any more serious aerial bombardment was slim. It's one of the remarkable things that made the fortitude of people in London and the southeast of England so remarkable.

As this photograph shows, a football match in August 1944 at Charlton Athletic's ground, the Valley, went ahead as normal with the exception of the Doodlebug spotters

positioned on the upper terraces to keep a watchful eye for any incoming missiles; Charlton Athletic lost to Reading by 8 goals to 2.

In all, over 9,000 Doodlebugs were fired against Britain but fewer than 40% managed to reach their target. Nevertheless, over 6,000 people were killed in the capital, and a further 18,000 were injured – and it was not only London that was hit. In the autumn the Luftwaffe found a new way of delivering V-Is and began launching them from specially converted Heinkel III bombers. On 24 December 1944 some 45 Doodlebugs were fired in this way from over the North Sea. Their target was Manchester; over 30 landed in the area, including half on Manchester itself.

A More Potent Threat

In an attempt to break the will of the British people and to cause a level of panic that would severely undermine the Government the Germans pressed into service the more deadly, because unstoppable, V-2 rockets in early September 1944. Weighing almost 13,000 kilograms these weapons came down from the stratosphere at 3,000 miles per hour – with no warning. These were psychologically more potent than the V-1s, but less effective against the civilian population, but only due to the fact that many fewer were fired against London and they had navigational

A V-2 rocket developed by Werner von Braun in the Second World War.

After one of the early V-2 attacks in September 1944 at Norwood Hospital in South London a nurse picks up some documents.

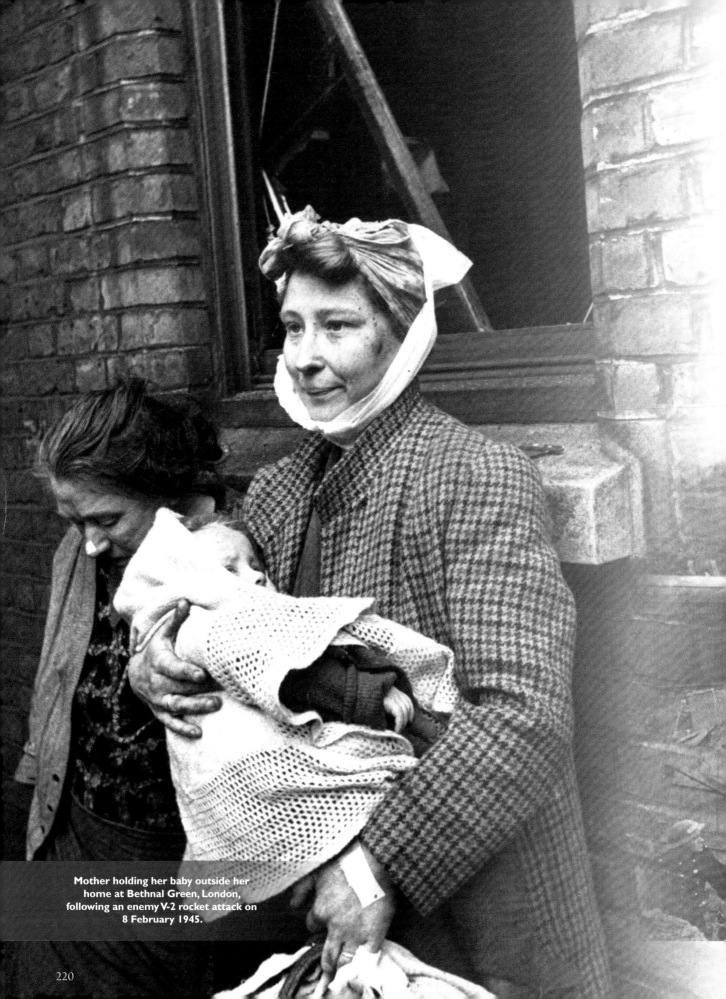

Mother holding her baby outside her home at Bethnal Green, London, following an enemy V-2 rocket attack on 8 February 1945.

and reliability problems. In all, around 2,700 people were killed and 6,000 injured by the 520 V-2s that hit London, with attacks continuing until 27 March 1945 when 34-year-old Mrs Ivy Millichamp became the last British civilian to die in an air raid. Such was the level of concern felt by the Government over the V-2 rockets that a plan for the evacuation of London was even considered. Thankfully, the threat of both the Doodlebug and the V-2 was put to rest when the advancing Allied armies in Europe captured the majority of the launch sites.

In the midst of the V-1 and V-2 attacks there was one welcome piece of news in early September:

"From September 17, when British Double Summer Time ends, window black-out will be replaced by "hall-lighting" over the whole country except in a few special coastal areas. Under the new requirement, windows other than skylights will only need to be curtained sufficiently to prevent objects inside the building from being distinguishable from the outside. This will enable ordinary peacetime curtains or blinds to be used, except the flimsiest kind, and from the streets a diffused light will be seen. On an air raid warning, complete obscuration will be required, either by drawing black out curtains or extinguishing the lights."

From 12 September 1944 daylight Fire Guard duties ended everywhere, while across most of Britain night duties were also suspended; in addition there were big cuts in Civil Defence duties.

The National Fire Service workshop in Ilford, Essex, was one of the last major casualties of the V-2 rocket attacks. A Norwich-bound steam locomotive passes in the background.

Free French!

On Wednesday 23 August a report of the liberation of Paris was broadcast on the lunchtime news of the BBC's French Service; on the BBC's Home Service at 1pm the news was read to the accompaniment of the bells of St Paul's. The liberation of Paris was symbolic since it gave people a sense of things moving towards a successful conclusion. Anxious to be there to share the moment, General de Gaulle had flown to France and was at the head of the column of troops that drove into the city. Three days later 40,000 people were amassed around Notre Dame Cathedral. Many were there to cheer the general, who had established the role of the Free French Forces in France. A BBC reporter was able to provide radio with a "first" – an assassination attempt live on air. In the background of the broadcast shots can clearly be heard. The reporter, Robert Reid, said: "Well, that was one of the most dramatic scenes I've ever seen. Just as General de Gaulle was about to enter the Cathedral of Notre Dame, firing started all over the place. I fell just near General de Gaulle and I managed to pick myself up. General de Gaulle was trying to control the crowds rushing into the cathedral. He walked straight ahead in what appeared to me to be a hail of fire from somewhere inside the cathedral, somewhere from the galleries up near the vaulted roof. But he went straight ahead without hesitation, his shoulders flung back, and walked right down the central aisle, even while the bullets were pouring around him…".

Some newspaper reports played down the attempt on 54-year-old de Gaulle's life. One even spoke of a "few stray bullets", and implied that it was not very serious. Throughout the weekend in the streets of Paris there were sporadic gun battles between small bands of concealed snipers and the Resistance. Even though the Germans had surrendered to General Leclerc there were still isolated groups of fanatical Nazis or the Darlan militia that carried on the fight. When shooting broke out at Notre Dame the Maquis turned their firepower on where the shots had come from, which included the gallery of the cathedral. As calm was restored four men, whom

Shortly after the liberation these US anti-aircraft guns guard the bridges over the Seine with the Eiffel Tower in the background.

one report described as "very obvious Germans", were marched out from inside Notre Dame with their hands above their heads. The shooting at the cathedral appeared to have been a signal for similar activities in other areas of Paris. The *Daily Telegraph*'s reporter said: "As we drove back to the Ritz Hotel, shots rang out in several streets. Despite these alarms, all Paris was in a holiday mood. The streets were filled with crowds of people all wearing their best, thousands of cycles were weaving in and out among the French and American army vehicles."

A BBC radio reporter speaking in France on 31 August 1944.

———— When Britain Went to War ————

Sunday Pictorial

August 27, 1944

PARIS FREE! —A City Mad with Delight

THIS IS PARIS. The first picture tells a story that will live for ever.

The cheers of a city freed from the shackles of tyranny ring out from this great picture taken by "Sunday Pictorial" cameraman Bill Turner in the Place de l'Opera.

It was a heartrending, touching spectacle. Hearts that had been tormented for four long, bitter years knew once again the joy of meeting free men. There was no halting, no reserve, the whole of Paris went mad with excitement.

PARIS FREE. Those two words flashed across the globe to bring a lump to the throats of the free people of the world. Stirring enough in print, but moving beyond words is the frenzied emotion that breathes from every face in this picture.

The price of the battle back to Paris has been heavy, but look again at this picture and know for all time that no price is too great to pay for gratitude such as this.

New Sensations Today

NEW sensations came in the great Balkans landslide early this morning.

Bulgaria announced that she is out of the war and told German troops to get out. And martial law has been declared in the German "protectorate" of Slovakia, where the Deputy Prime Minister went on the radio this morning to declare that "enemy" parachutists were being dropped.

He called on the people "not to betray the Germans" but to stand by them faithfully—an admission that he knows the extent of anti-German feeling in this detached part of the old Czechoslovakia.

He gave no news as to where the parachutists came from, but they may be Czech troops who have been under training in Russia.

In France, too, the Germans are heading for another disaster—as told on the back page—for they are now being pursued across the Seine by American armoured columns and are even rushing to get out of Belgium.

DEMOBILISATION PLAN FIXED: P.4

How Our Fighting Men Will Come Back Home—EXCLUSIVE

They Had No Pity to Spare

Every woman in Britain who looks at this picture will be shocked. This girl had been the lover of a German. He was the father of the baby she carries down the street of Chartres after she had been branded by having her head shaved. There was not a sympathetic glance, nothing but grins and jeers. The only excuse for the people is that they remember each other's sufferings at the hands of the invaders and they have no pity to spare.

Allied cars in a Paris street parked alongside cars of the Free French Resistance movement, which have FFI, painted on the side.

Early morning scene in the Fish Market in Manchester in November 1944 as housewives rush for surplus fish.

Running on Empty

Fuel was rationed from September 1939, but this did not prove a great hardship for the average British family; car ownership was a fraction of what it is today and so the impact on daily life was much less. In 1930 there were about a million cars in Britain and this number had doubled by the time war broke out; interestingly, the number of cars roughly matched the number of telephones. But fuel was not only used in private cars; lorries and delivery vehicles were consumers too. Rationing of petrol for cars finally ended on 26 May 1950, to the jubilation of the owners of around 3.5 million motorcars.

In March 1945, the Ministry of War Transport Committee on Road Safety published a report relating to war and road casualties in Great Britain. Between September 1939 and March 1945 the number of deaths and serious injuries on the roads of Britain was 158,000. Deaths and serious injuries from enemy attacks of all descriptions, 140,000.

Fitting blackout shields to the headlamps of a car. Naturally, the blackout contributed to road accidents.

A new type of animal ambulance was designed by a Mr Paddle of Isleworth in 1943; he presented it to the National ARP Animals Society for their use.

According to *Hansard*, in 1943 a total of 5,796 people were killed on the roads and 116,740 were injured. In the first 11 months of 1944, the corresponding numbers were 5,807 and 112,833. The death toll on Britain's roads in 2008 was 2,943, the lowest since 1926.

Women garage workers filling a van with petrol.

Women queue in London to receive their supply of coal in February 1945.

One Lump
or Two?

Of much more significance was the shortage of domestic coal. Before war broke out virtually every home in Britain used coal as its principal form of heating, which meant the demand for that fuel was huge. The requirements of industry for electricity, which was largely generated by coal-fired power stations, coupled with the shortage of miners throughout the war meant that the scramble for domestic coal remained a constant problem throughout the cold winter months of every year of the war.

In 1943 the solution to manpower shortages was aided by the formation of the "Bevin Boys", young men who were conscripted to work down the mines through a scheme created by the wartime Minister for Labour

Women scavenging for pieces of coal amongst the slag at a pit near Gorton in Manchester, in January 1945. Some of the women were factory workers who had taken the day off to get their fuel.

and National Service, Ernest Bevin. Despite the dangerous and unpleasant conditions in which they worked many were branded as cowards for not going off to fight. For many years the efforts of the 48,000 Bevin Boys during the Second World War were all but forgotten; not one got a medal.

Langley pit lads in September 1943.

The Propaganda War

RAF ground crew load propaganda leaflets into the bomb bay of a Vickers Wellington bomber in 1944; these were dropped on Germany throughout the war. The Nazis did the same to Britain. Because of the flimsy nature of the paper very few of these leaflets have survived. The leaflets pictured here warn of bombing raids on Germany in October 1944.

The Reich Chancellery Gardens in Berlin, where the bodies of Hitler and Eva Braun were burned.

The Fall of Berlin

At the beginning of April 1945 the Russian Army was 20 to 30 miles from Berlin while the main Allied force was 200 miles away in the west; and so, despite the Russians facing stiffer opposition than the American and British forces, the "race for Berlin" was in fact no contest. Despite much urging by Churchill, Eisenhower did not set Montgomery free to make the final dash to Berlin; the Supreme Commander ordered the 21st Army Group to halt at the River Elbe – they were some 60 or so miles from Berlin, and the Russians still hadn't made it. Churchill cabled Roosevelt arguing that it was important that the British and Americans got there first, but on 11 April Roosevelt

disagreed in a reply to Churchill, just as he had done over the zoning of Germany at the Yalta conference two months earlier. It was the US President's last significant act of the war: Franklin D Roosevelt died on 12 April.

The news of the President Roosevelt's death was keenly felt by many in Britain, where he was recognized as a true friend, at a time when the country was desperately in need of one. His death had nothing to do with the order to halt at the Elbe issued by Eisenhower, who was still being urged by Patton to let the 21st Army Group go all the way to Berlin. While some have seen this decision to call a halt as a mistake Eisenhower always insisted that it was to save lives. The Russians suffered in excess of 300,000 casualties during that last push to Berlin; the Supreme Commander's view was simple and pragmatic. Why risk the lives of soldiers to capture Berlin when it was going to be in the Soviet zone once the fighting had finished (this arrangement had been agreed at Yalta)? At the same time, Eisenhower was under orders from Washington not to take the city and risk the wrath of Russia being brought to bear on America. This was another example of history's "what ifs".

On St George's Day, 23 April, the Russians finally broke through the bitter resistance on the eastern outskirts of Berlin. Two days later Russian and British troops finally met up – but not in Berlin. Torgau, where the armies met, is about 100 miles southwest of Berlin, and fierce fighting had continued there. Hitler had declared Berlin the front line and those soldiers who remained in the

Two Russian soldiers talking to American soldiers as the first American tanks arrived in Berlin.

Berliners make their way home in a horse-drawn cart with the ruins of the engineering college behind them.

city were fighting for their lives. On 28 April, with the Red Army at the gates of his chancellery, the Führer married his lover, Eva Braun, and named Admiral Dönitz as his successor. Two days later he shot himself, his wife poisoned herself, as did Goebbels and his wife who were with Hitler in his bunker – but not before poisoning their six children.

The BBC interrupted its normal programming on 1 May to announce the Führer's death; this followed hard on the heals of a broadcast made on German radio at 9.40pm which said, somewhat euphemistically, "Adolf Hitler has fallen this afternoon at his Command Post in the Reich Chancellery fighting to his last breath against Bolshevism, and for Germany." Immediately preceding the announcement on Hamburg Radio Wagner's

Götterdämmerung (*The Twilight of the Gods*) was played. Admiral Dönitz broadcast immediately after the news of Hitler's death was announced and finished his speech by saying:

"German Soldiers do your duty. The very life of our people is at stake."

The following day fighting in Berlin continued and at around 10.15pm on 2 May programmes were again interrupted on the radio to announce the fall of Berlin.

Troops of the British 7th Armoured Division led by the 11th Hussars enter Berlin.

The desolation in Berlin.

Daily Mirror

No. 12,906 Wednesday, May 2, 1945 ONE PENNY
Registered at G.P.O. as a Newspaper.

"GERMANY WILL BATTLE ON"

HITLER DEAD

Killed in Berlin, says new Fuehrer, Admiral Doenitz

HITLER was killed in action yesterday afternoon, according to a broadcast from Hamburg at 10.30 last night.

His successor is Rear-Admiral Doenitz, the C.-in-C. of the German Navy, who made the announcement himself.

Doenitz said: "The Fuehrer has fallen at his command post in Berlin. He fell for Germany."

Adolf Hitler, leader of the Nazi Reich since January 30, 1933, the world's chief criminal, now dead at the age of fifty-six.

This is Doenitz

Admiral Doenitz, who directed the U-boat war, and who has stolen himself head of the Nazi Reich

"MY FIRST TASK," SAID DOE-NITZ, "IS TO SAVE THE GERMAN PEOPLE FROM DES-TRUCTION BY BOL-SHEVISM. IF ONLY FOR THIS TASK THE STRUGGLE WILL CONTINUE.

"Give me your confidence. Do your duty. Keep order. Only in this way shall we be able to prevent collapse.

The German announcement came just as the House of Commons rose.

After a roll of drums, Hamburg radio said:

"It is reported from the Fuehrer's headquarters that our Fuehrer, Adolf Hitler, has fallen this afternoon at his command post in the Reich Chancellery fighting to the last breath against Bolshevism and for Germany.

"On April 30 the Fuehrer appointed Grand Admiral Doenitz as his successor.

"Our new Fuehrer will speak to the German people.

The last reference to Hitler was in yesterday's

Continued on Back Page

'Lay down your arms' —Graziani to his Army

MARSHAL GRAZIANI, commander of the Ligurian Army, who was captured by the Allies in Italy, said this over Rome radio last night:

To Italian and German troops in Liguria, lay down your arms. For several days the German Surrender main in Italy has not been offered. Under the circumstances I took over the personal responsibilities of unconditional surrender to the U.S. Command on April 29. Further resistance would not only be useless, but also dangerous for yourself.

DANES ARE TAKING OVER FROM THE GERMAN ARMY

THE Danes are taking control in their own country again, Danish police in full uniform are again patrolling the streets of several towns from which the Germans have withdrawn without incident.

This sensational news was released by British United Press from Copenhagen, capital of Denmark, last night.

The Danish and German authorities, it was stated, are negotiating an agreement for the relinquishment of the Danish police all over the country.

Count Folke Bernadotte was yesterday reported to

have flown from Denmark with a German - Swedish agreement for the surrender of Nazi troops in both Denmark and Norway.

Danish underground source reported that the movement of German troops from North to South Denmark has already begun.

Other sources believed that the Swedes had proposed the the Huns had called—that the Germans Army in Norway should go to Sweden to be disarmed there.

The Nazis want to get their troops into Sweden before

CIVIL SERVANTS ARE ASKING FOR HIGHER PAY

WAGE increases and reduced hours are urged in resolutions tabled for the two-day Annual Conference of the Society of Civil Servants next week in London.

A general atmosphere of unusual incareasing is sought in one resolution from the Midlands, which also urges a five-day working week for the Civil Service when hostilities cease.

'Wait' is Churchill's tip to the Commons

MR. CHURCHILL told the Commons yesterday that he had no special statement to make about the war situation in Europe, but if information reached the Government he would tell the House.

"It was not his idea that information should be kept here until the exact conclusion of all the particular issues."

Snowfire BEAUTY MAKERS

Snowfire Girls: MARGARET

Margaret is essentially a man's girl. She likes the drinks that men like; she appreciates good cooking and the finer points of most sports. And, as she is never separated from her Snowfire Beauty Makers, she is always good to look at.

For ever and a Date!

CREAMS • POWDER • LIPSTICK

The Brandenburg Gate in Berlin immediately after the fall of the city.

Victory in Europe Day

On Monday 7 May at around 4.30pm news came in from General Eisenhower's HQ about the signing of the surrender terms. At 7.45pm the Ministry of Information gave permission for the following statement to be broadcast:

"This is the BBC Home Service. We are interrupting programmes to make the following announcement. It is understood that in accordance with arrangements between the three great powers an official announcement will be broadcast by the Prime Minister at 3 o'clock tomorrow Tuesday afternoon the 8th of May. In view of this fact tomorrow, Tuesday, will be treated as Victory in Europe day. and will be regarded as a holiday. The day following Wednesday the 9th of May will also be a holiday. His Majesty the King will broadcast to the people of the British Empire and Commonwealth tomorrow Tuesday at 9p.m. British double summer time." – **John Snagge, BBC Home Service, 7.45pm, 7 May 1945**

21 ARMY GROUP

PERSONAL MESSAGE
FROM THE C-IN-C

(To be read out to all Troops)

1. On this day of victory in Europe I feel I would like to speak to all who have served and fought with me during the last few years. What I have to say is very simple, and quite short.

2. I would ask you all to remember those of our comrades who fell in the struggle. They gave their lives that others might have freedom, and no man can do more than that. I believe that He would say to each one of them:

   "Well done, thou good and faithful servant."

3. And we who remain have seen the thing through to the end; we all have a feeling of great joy and thankfulness that we have been preserved to see this day.

   We must remember to give the praise and thankfulness where it is due:

   "This is the Lord's doing, and it is marvellous in our eyes."

4. In the early days of this war the British Empire stood alone against the combined might of the axis powers. And during those days we suffered some great disasters; but we stood firm: on the defensive, but striking blows where we could. Later we were joined by Russia and America; and from then onwards the end was in no doubt. Let us never forget what we owe to our Russian and American allies; this great allied team has achieved much in war; may it achieve even more in peace.

5. Without doubt, great problems lie ahead; the world will not recover quickly from the upheaval that has taken place; there is much work for each one of us.

   I would say that we must face up to that work with the same fortitude that we faced up to the worst days of this war. It may be that some difficult times lie ahead for our country, and for each one of us personally. If it happens thus, then our discipline will pull us through; but we must remember that the best discipline implies the subordination of self for the benefit of the community.

6. It has been a privilege and an honour to command this great British Empire team in western Europe. Few commanders can have had such loyal service as you have given me. I thank each one of you from the bottom of my heart.

7. And so let us embark on what lies ahead full of joy and optimism. We have won the German war. Let us now win the peace.

8. Good luck to you all, wherever you may be.

B. L. Montgomery

Germany,
May, 1945.

Field-Marshal,
C.-in-C.,
21 Army Group.

St Paul's Cathedral floodlit during the VE day celebrations.

It's a Party!

Piccadilly Circus, London.

Pipe band march down The Mound in Edinburgh.

A street party in the Newton Heath district of Manchester on 8 May 1945.

A German figure is burnt at a VE day street party.

Crowds cheer Prime Minister Winston Churchill after his victory speech from a balcony in Whitehall.

The King's Speech

Today we give thanks to Almighty God for a great deliverance.

Speaking from our empire's oldest capital city, war-battered but never for one moment daunted or dismayed, speaking from London, I ask you to join with me in that act of thanksgiving.

Germany, the enemy who drove all Europe into war, has been finally overcome. In the Far East we have yet to deal with the Japanese, a determined and cruel foe. To this we shall turn with the utmost resolve and with all our resources. But at this hour when the dreadful shadow of war has passed far from our hearths and homes in these islands, we may at last make one pause for thanksgiving and then turn our thoughts to the task all over the world which peace in Europe brings with it.

Prime Minister Winston Churchill joins the Royal Family on the balcony at Buckingham Palace on VE day. Left to right: Princess Elizabeth, Queen Elizabeth, Winston Churchill, King George VI and Princess Margaret.

Daily Mirror

Tuesday, May 8, 1945 ONE PENNY
No. 12,911 Registered at G.P.O. as a Newspaper

VE-DAY !

IT'S OVER IN THE WEST

TODAY is VE-Day—the day for which the British people have fought and endured five years, eight months and four days of war.

With unconditional surrender accepted by Germany's last remaining leaders, the war in Europe is over except for the actions of fanatical Nazis in isolated pockets, such as Prague.

The Prime Minister will make an official announcement—in accordance with arrangements between Britain, Russia and the U.S.—at 3 o'clock this afternoon.

ALL TODAY AND TO-MORROW ARE PUBLIC HOLIDAYS IN BRITAIN, IN CELEBRATION OF OUR VICTORY.

We also remember and salute with gratitude and pride the men and women who suffered and died to make triumph possible for men still battling in the East against another enemy who is still in the field.

War winners broadcast today

You will hear the voices of the King, Field-Marshals Montgomery and Alexander and General Eisenhower when they broadcast over the B.B.C. Home Service today.

After the King's speech at 9 p.m., and reported from 9 by the news bulletin, comes "Victory Report," a special programme which will combine the recorded voices of war leaders with the famous personalities of the war years.

In addition to all this the B.B.C. Home programmes, which instead of 9 are to continue to an hour earlier in the evening, will sustain the air from Piccadilly Circus and Trafalgar Square (6.30 a.m.) to the King.

VE-SCENE TRAFALGAR SQUARE

"Daily Mirror" Reporter

It was a high old time in Trafalgar Square last night. Everybody wanted to climb something. This party of Wrens and A.T.S soldiers embroidered in clambering up to the lions, merry policemen—

London had joy night

Let us remember those who will not come back: their constancy and courage in battle, their sacrifice and endurance in the face of a merciless enemy; let us remember the men in all the services, the women in all the services, who have laid down their lives.

We have come to the end of our tribulation and they are not with us at the moment of our rejoicing...

The morning after the night before.

Clement Attlee and his wife after Labour's
election victory.

Labour Landslide!

Two months after VE day there were elections in Britain
in which the radio played an important part. It was not
the first time that the wireless had been used by the

political parties, and there was a formula in existence for
how much time should be allotted to each party. For four
weeks both the Home and the Forces programmes carried
20- to 30-minute speeches by the party leaders. However,
whereas in the past the BBC had seen its role as purely a
purveyor of electoral news it now entered a new phase by
offering comment on the political process. Things would
never ever be the same again.

When Britain Went to War

Clement Atlee led the Labour Party to a landslide victory and the Party's first overall working majority. Polling day was 5 July, with some votes being delayed until as late as 19 July. Labour secured 393 MPs, with the Conservatives getting 197 and the Liberals just 12 seats. This was a major shock to the Tories, whose leader, Winston Churchill, had after all led the country to victory. For many voters the fact that not just Atlee but also Herbert Morrison and Ernest Bevin had shown real skill in overseeing domestic departments during the war – all departments that mattered to returning servicemen and those wanting to see Britain rebuilt after the war – is what gave Labour their landslide.

Winston Churchill campaigning in Liverpool in the General Election.

A deputation arriving at Parliament during the election campaign.

VJ Day

Three months after the victory in Europe and following the Labour Party's landslide victory, the new Prime Minister, Clement Atlee, was the one to give the news of the surrender of the Japanese. Shortly after noon on 15 August Emperor Hirohito formally surrendered.

The surrender followed the US Airforce's dropping of an atomic bomb on Hiroshima on 6 August, in which

The VJ day victory parade in Newcastle.

78,000 were killed; three days later the A-bomb fell on Nagasaki, causing a further 35,000 to die. On 10 August, the day after the Nagasaki bomb was dropped, the Japanese began peace negotiations.

Daily Mirror **building decorated to celebrate VJ day.**

Index

These young women and a sailor appear to have slept out in Trafalgar Square following the VE day celebrations. While one woman prepares her hair, the sailor washes in the fountain, his uniform and flag crisply folded at his side. Their composure and orderliness hint at a generation of people who have withstood the trials of war but are still capable of retaining their dignity under the most testing circumstances.

This book is dedicated to my mother, Bettina, who, as a teenager, worked in London during the 'Doodlebug Summer' and later at Croydon airport. To my father, John, who was called up at the end of the war, joining the Essex Regiment and guarded German POWs. To Douglas Wooldridge, my uncle, who served with RAF Bomber Command and flew on raids over Germany, was shot down, taken prisoner, and is today still travelling the world; it's also for his late wife Mary who was a WAAF. They, along with millions of British men and women, whether as members of the Armed Forces or as civilians 'did their bit' – *When Britain Went To War*.

Thanks to Fergus McKenna and David Scipps along with all the guys at Mirrorpix; particularly John Mead, who came up with some 'crackers'. Kevin Gardner for his superb design work; Elizabeth Stone for her editorial skills and Becky Ellis for proofreading and keeping me on the straight and narrow. Thanks to my agent Paul Moreton at Bell, Lomax, Moreton and a big thank you to Jeremy Yates-Round at Haynes Publishing who makes it all happen.